INTRODUCTION

Welcome to the world of digital publishing ~ the book you now hold in your hand, while unchanged from the original **1967** edition, was printed using the latest state of the art digital technology. The advent of print-on-demand has forever changed the publishing process, never has information been so accessible and it is our hope that this book serves your informational needs for years to come. If this is your first exposure to digital publishing, we hope that you are pleased with the results. Many more titles of interest to the classic automobile and motorcycle enthusiast, collector and restorer are available via our website at **www.VelocePress.com**. We hope that you find this title as interesting as we do.

NOTE FROM THE PUBLISHER

The information presented is true and complete to the best of our knowledge. All recommendations are made without any guarantees on the part of the author or the publisher, who also disclaim all liability incurred with the use of this information.

TRADEMARKS

We recognize that some words, model names and designations, for example, mentioned herein are the property of the trademark holder. We use them for identification purposes only. This is not an official publication.

INFORMATION ON THE USE OF THIS PUBLICATION

This manual is an invaluable resource for the classic **Honda** motorcycle enthusiast and a must have for owners interested in performing their own maintenance. However, in today's information age we are constantly subject to changes in common practice, new technology, availability of improved materials and increased awareness of chemical toxicity. As such, it is advised that the user consult with an experienced professional prior to undertaking any procedure described herein. While every care has been taken to ensure correctness of information, it is obviously not possible to guarantee complete freedom from errors or omissions or to accept liability arising from such errors or omissions. Therefore, any individual that uses the information contained within, or elects to perform or participate in do-it-yourself repairs or modifications acknowledges that there is a risk factor involved and that the publisher or its associates cannot be held responsible for personal injury or property damage resulting from the use of the information or the outcome of such procedures.

It is important that the reader recognizes that any instructions may refer to either the right-hand or left-hand sides of the vehicle or the components and that the directions are followed carefully. One final word of advice, this publication is intended to be used as a reference guide, and when in doubt the reader should consult with a qualified expert.

© 2007 Veloce Enterprises Inc., San Antonio, TX 78230, USA

All rights reserved. This work may not be reproduced or transmitted in any form without the express written consent of the publisher.

ANNOUNCEMENT

We are happy to reproduce this Shop Manual and Owner's Handbook covering the 250 to 300cc range of the extremely popular Honda motorcycle line. This book has been published in response to numerous and increasing demands from many customers; including motorcycle dealers, bookstore and newsstand managers, motorcycling enthusiasts, and — of course — Honda owners and prospective owners.

Two further books on Honda motorcycles have been made available by Floyd Clymer Publications. One covers Honda machines in the 50cc category, with special emphasis on the Super Cub (C 100) and Sport Cub (C 110) models. The other book covers the Honda intermediate range: 125cc and 150cc machines.

These books were originally printed in Japan and translated in that country. There are some expressions that differ from our own but we have left the wording exactly as it appears in the original books.

Floyd Clymer

HONDA MOTOR CO., LTD.

HONDA 250 MODEL C72

HONDA 250 MODEL CS72

HONDA 250 MODEL CB72

MAINTENANCE STANDARDS	C72·77 1
	CB72·77 15

DISASSEMBLY & ASSEMBLY 41

CONSTRUCTION 89

ELECTRIC EQUIPMENT 133

TROUBLE SHOOTING 175

PREFACE

This Shop Manual contains general data and information, and procedures relative to vehicle maintenance, over-haul and repairs for the models covered by Honda 250 and Honda 300 equivalent to Model C72·C77, CB72·CB77, CS72·CS77.

Therefore, information in this manual will be suitable instruction for servicemen and mechanics of Honda to assist them to efficiently service and repair these machines.

Now, in this case, mechanical arrangement means to repair a vehicle when it is out of order and restore it to the ordinary state as well as to prevent it from any trouble by periodically inspecting the vehicle.

The contains of this book are divided into five chapters, including main standards, disassembly-assembly, construction, wiring diagram and trouble shooting.

Each chapters are separated into sections. Disassembly-assembly (the 2nd chapter) is divided into 2 sections – Engine and Frame. The section of Engine is described both model C72·77, CB72·77, but that of Frame is done only model CB72·77.

In regard to the Frame of model C72·77, please refer to the previously published Shop Manual for Honda 125·150.

An effort has been made to produce a manual avoiding fundamental principle and theory by explaining the actual mechanism.

Special emphasis has been placed on illustrations and charts to make it easy for the service man to understand without reading every line. We hope this will be of some use to you.

This manual will be revised without notice.

HONDA MOTOR CO., LTD.
TECHNICAL SECTION
EXPORT DEPARTMENT
No. 5-5, Yaesu-cho, Chuo-ku,
Tokyo, Japan

MAINTENANCE STANDARDS, C72·77

For maintenance operation for HONDA 250·300, Maintenance Standards, specification and dimension are listed hereafter for reference.

EXPLANATION:

Maintenance Items Items to be inspected, service-wise.

Standard Value This indicates the manufacturer's standard size or the standard size after newly assembling or adjusting, and shows the size-limit of completed part in the permissible limit of adjustment.

Repairing Limit Unusable wear limit of parts requiring correction or replacement, function-wise.

Remarks Unmarked numbers are run unit and inch unit shown underneath, and others according to the unit indicated.

UNIT IN CHART:

Unmarked numbers are m/m unit and inch unit shown underneath, and others according to the unit indicated.

CONTENTS

1. GENERAL PERFORMANCE 1

2. ENGINE
   - A. Cylinder, Cylinder Head 1
   - B. Crank Shaft (Piston, Connecting Rod) 2
   - C. Cam, Timing and Valve 3
   - D. Upper Crank Case 5
   - E. Clutch, L. Crank Case Cover 5
   - F. Transmission 6
   - G. Magneto, Contact Point 7
   - H. Oil Pump, Oil Separator 8
   - I. Kick, R. Crank Case Cover 8
   - J. Under Crank Case and Change 8

3. FRAME
   - A. Handle 9
   - B. Front Cushion 9
   - C. Front Fork, Steering, Tank 10
   - D. Frame Body 10
   - E. Saddle, Stand 11
   - F. Rear Fork, Chain Case 11
   - G. Rear Cushion 11
   - H. Front Wheel 11
   - I. Rear Wheel 12

MAINTENANCE STANDARDS (Model C72)

This maintenance standards is listed only about the data of Model C72. In this list, dimentions without units indicate "mm" (upper step) and "inch" (down step), and others according to the units indicated.

1. GENERAL PERFORMANCE

Item		Standard	Repairing Limit	Remarks
Compression pressure		8.5 kg/cm^2 120.87 lb/in^2	7.0 99.54 lb/in^2	Check with kick
Fuel consumption		42~45 km/ℓ 26.04~27.90 mile/ℓ	29 17.98	35 km/h (21.7 mile/h)
Lubricant consumption		120 cc/1000 km or less 120 cc/620 mile	200/1000 more 200/620 mile	
Max. speed		130 km/h 80.60 mile/h	90 less 55.80 mile	The posture is leaning forward one thirds of the body

2. ENGINE

A. Cylinder, Cylinder Head

Item		Standard	Repairing Limit	Remarks
Cylinder	Inner dia.	53.99~54.00 2.1255~2.1259	54.1 more 2.129	
	Max. out of round	within 0.001	0.05 more 0.00019	
	Taper	within 0.001	0.05 more 0.00019	
Over size of cylinder	Over size	0.25 0.00984		3 category of 0.25 (0.0098) over size
Cylinder head valve sheet	Width	1.0~1.5 0.0393~0.0590	2.0 more 0.0787	
	Angle	45°		
Compression ratio		8.3 0.326		The capacity of the combustion chamber, 16.94 cc
Cylinder head gasket surface	Flatness	within 0.03 0.0011	0.06 more 0.0023	
Cylinder head gasket	Thickness	1.0~1.1 0.039~0.043		In case of binding
Cylinder stut nut	Tightness	2.1 kgm 15.189 ft lb		

B. Crank Shaft (Piston, Connecting Rod)

Item		Standard	Repairing Limit	Remarks
Piston	Top diameter	53.55~53.60 2.108~2.110	53.5 less 2.106	The progressive direction of the lower parts of skirt
	Max. dia.	$54^{+0}_{-0.02}=D$	53.9 less 2.112	
	Out of round	D−(0.14~0.16)=d D−(0.005~0.006)=d		
Piston & cylinder	Min. clearance	0	0.1 more 0.0039	
Piston pin	Dia.	15.0~15.0006 0.59~0.5907	15.05 more 0.5925	
Piston over size	Over size	0.25 0.0098		3 category of 0.25 (0.0098) over size
	Taper	D−0.08d−0.08 D−0.0031d−0.003		
Top・2nd ring	Thickness	2.4~2.6 0.094~0.102	2.3 less 0.0905	
	Width	1.780~1.795 0.0700~0.0778	1.7 less 0.0669	
	Tension	0.75~1.05kg (top) 0.70~1.00kg (2nd) 1.653~2.315 lb 1.543~2.205 lb	0.6 kg less 1.3230 less	Tangential tension In case of binding
	End gap	0.15~0.35 0.0059~0.0137	0.8 more 0.314	
Top・2nd ring & ring groove	Clearance	0.01~0.04 0.0003~0.00015	0.1 more 0.0039	
Oil ring	Thickness	2.4~2.6 0.0944~0.1023	2.0 less 0.0787	
	Width	2.780~2.795 0.1094~0.1100	2.7 less 0.10629	
	Tension	0.7~0.9 kg 1.5435~1.9845 lb	0.5 less 1.1025 lb	Tangential tension
	End gap	0.1~0.3 0.0039~0.0118	0.8 more 0.0314	In case of binding
Oil ring & ring groove	Clearance	0.01~0.04 0.0003~0.0015	0.1 more 0 0039	
Piston over size	Over size	0.25 0.0098		3 category of 0.25 (0.0098) over size
Piston pin	Out. dia.	14.994~15.0 0.5903~0.5905	14.95 less 0.5885	
	Total length	45.5~45.7 1.7913~1.7992		

Item		Standard	Repairing Limit	Remarks
Piston pin & piston	Clearance	0~0.012 0~0.0004	0.05 more 0.00196	In cold, push in softly by fingers
Connecting rod small end	In. dia.	15.016~15.043 0.5911~0.5922	15.08 more 0.5936	
Con. rod small end & piston pin	Clearance	0.016~0.049 0.0006~0.0019	0.08 more 0.0031	
Con. rod small end	Swing		3.0 more 0.118	Max. amplitude to axial direction of crank pin
Lower end of con. rod	Axial clearance	0.07~0.33 0.0027~0.012	0.5 more 0.0196	
	Diagonal clearance	0.006~0.016	0.05 more	
Big end·small end of con. rod	Amount of parallel	within 0.02 0.00078	over 0.1 0.0039	At length of 100 mm (3.93 in)
	Distortion	within 0.02 0.00078	over 0.1 0.0039	At length of 100 mm (3.93 in)
Baranser weight crankpin	Out. dia.	24.99~25.00 0.9838~0.9842	24.95 or less 0.9822	
R. L. crank shaft	Dia. of shaft	30.82~30.86 1.213~1.215	30.6 or less 1.204	
Crank shaft bearing	Axial clearance	0.005 0.00019	over 0.1 0.0039	Center bearing
	Radial clearance	0.014~0.016 0.0005~0.0006	over 0.05 0.0019	
Crank shaft combination	Max. swing	0.03 less 0.0011	over 0.1 0.0039	In case of supporting center bearing, the swing of both ends
Cam chain	Overall length	723.0~723.8 28.46~28.49	over 728 28.66	

C. Cam · Timing and Valve Mechanism

Item		Standard	Repairing Limit	Remarks
Ex. In. valve guide	In. dia.	7.0~7.01 0.2755~0.2759	over 7.05 0.2775	
Ex. valve	Overall length	88.65~88.85 3.490~3.498	88.2 or less 3.472	
	Out. dia. of stem	6.97~6.98 0.2744~0.2748	6.95 or less 0.273	
	Thickness of head	1.0 0.03937	0.5 or less 0.001968	
In. valve	Overall length	89.18~89.38 3.511~3.518	88.7 or less 3.492	
	Out. dia. of stem	6.97~6.98 0.2744~0.2748	6.95 or less 0.273	

Item		Standard	Repairing Limit	Remarks
Ex. In. valve	Thickness of head	1.0 0.03936	0.5 or less 0.0019	
	Width	1.0~1.5 0.0393~0.059	over 2 0 0.0787	
Ex. valve stem and guide	Clearance	0.02~0.04 0.0007~0.0015	over 0.08 0.0031	
In. valve stem and guide	Clearance	0.01~0.03 0.00039~0.0011	over 0.07 0.00275	
Valve spring outer	Free length	43.82 1.725	42.3 or less 1.665	
	Tension	11.6~12.4 kg 24.2~25.8 kg 25.57~27.3 lb 53.36~56.8 lb		At 34.5 mm (1.35) of binding length At 27.5 mm (1.08) of max. lift
Valve spring outer	Decline	within 1. 0.03937	1.5 more 0.059	
Valve spring inner	Free length	34.66 1.364	33.4 less 1.314	
	Tension	3.9~4.3 kg 14.5~15.5 kg 8.59~9.48 lb 31.97~34.17 lb		At 31.5 mm (1.24) of binding length At 24.5 mm (0.96) of max. lift
	Decline	within 1. 0.0393	1.5 more 0.059	
Cam shaft	Shaft dia.	19.98~19.99 0.786~0.787	19.95 less 0.785	
	Bend of shaft	within 0.01 0.0003	0.05 more 0.0019	
	Height of cam	26.98~27.02 0.01062~0.01063	26.7 less 0.0105	
Cam shaft and bearing of journal	Clearance	(−) (+) 0.003~0.03 0.00011~0.0011	0.08 more 0.0031	
Valve timing Ex. [at 1.1 mm (0.043) of Lift length]	Opening angle	before lower dead point 25°	±5°	P. 6 cam
	Closing angle	after upper dead point 10°	±5°	Non-clearance
Valve timing In. [at 1.1 mm (0.043) of Lift length]	Opening angle	before upper dead point 10°	±5°	P. 6 cam
	Closing angle	after lower dead point 25°	±5°	Non-clearance
Cam sprocket	Bottom diameter	74.766 2.943	74.2 less 2.922	
Rocker arm	To fix steps on slipper face		0.3 more 0.0118	In case of having some trouble on slipper surface

Item		Standard	Repairing Limit	Remarks
Rocker arm crankpin	In. dia.	13.0~13.027 0.511~0.522	13.1 more 0.515	
	Out. dia.	12.966~12.984 0.510~0.511	12.9 less 0.5078	
	Clearance to rocker arm	0.16~0.061 0.0006~0.0024	0.1 more 0.0039	
Ex. In. valve adjust	Tappet clearance	0.09~0.11 0.0035~0.0043	out of standard	Cool state
Cam chain tensioner spring	Free length	73 2.874	70 less 2.755	
	Tension	16.0~16.2 kg 35.28~35.71 lb	10 less 22.05	
Cam chain tensioner roller	Out. dia.	59.2~59.8 2.33~2.35	58.5 less 2.303	Without injury of rubber

D. Upper Crank Case

Item		Standard	Repairing Limit	Remarks
Hole, shift drum	In dia.	34.0~34.02 1.338~1.339	34.2 more 1.346	
	In dia. of axle	12.0~12.01 0.472~0.473	12.2 more 0.4803	
Cam chain guide roller pin	Out. dia.	13.966~13.984 0.549~0.550	13.9 less 0.547	
Chain guide roller	In. dia.	14.0~14.01 0.5511~0.5518	14.1 more 0.5551	

E. Clutch · L. Crank Case Cover

Item		Standard	Repairing Limit	Remarks
Clutch center	In. dia.	25.0~25.021 21.0~21.084 0.984~0.985 0.826~0.830	24.9 20.9 less 0.980 0.822	
	Out-round swing	within 0.1 0.0039	0.2 more 0.0078	
Primary drive sprocket	Bottom diameter	39.11~39.21 1.5397~1.5436	38.3 less 1.5078	
Clutch friction disc	Thickness	4.8~4.9 0.1889~0.1929	4.4 less 0.1732	
	Strain	within 0.2 0.0078	0.5 more 0.0196	

Item		Standard	Repairing Limit	Remarks
Clutch plate	Strain	within 0.2 0.0078	0.5 more 0.0196	
	Width of hook	13.7~13.8 0.5393~0.5433	13.0 less 0.5118	
Teeth and outer of clutch pressure plate	Rotary play	within 0.2 0.0078	0.8 more 0.0314	
Clutch spring	Free length	33.4 1.3149	32.4 less 1.2755	
	Tension	15.3~16.7 kg 19.8 kg 33.736~36.823 lb 43.659 lb	15.0 less (23.075)	At 25 mm (0.98) of binding length At 23 mm (0.90) of max. lift

F. Transmission

Item		Standard	Repairing Limit	Remarks
Mission case lubricating oil	Capacity	1.5 ℓ 0.396 gal U.S.	out of standard	In crank and mission
Main shaft	Out. dia.	24.959~24.98 0.9826~0.9834	24.9 less 0.980	
Main shaft and M2 gear	Clearance	0.07~0.074	0.1 more 0.0039	
Axial direction of main shaft	Clearance	0.1~0.75 0.0039~0.0295	1.2 more 0.0472	
Turning direction of M3 gear	Clearance	0.03~0.078	0.1 more 0.0039	
Teeth surface of gear relating to mission	Axis play	0.089~0.178	0.2 more 0.0078	
Top gear bush 18φ	In. dia.	18.0~18.018 0.708~0.709	18.1 more 0.712	
Top gear bush 20.5φ	In. dia.	20.5~20.52 0.8070~0.8079	20.6 more 0.811	
Top gear bush & main shaft	Clearance	0.04~0.082	0.1 more 0.0039	
Drive sprocket	Bottom dia.	71.5~71.51 65.649~65.776 2.814~2.815 2.584~2.589	70.5 less 64.7 less 2.77 2.54	
	Rotary play	0.03~0.078	0.5 more 0.019	Spline parts
Primary driven sprocket	Bottom dia.	136.06~136.16 5.356~5.360	135.3 less 5.326	
Main shaft & top gear bearing	Axis play	0.005	0 1 more 0.0039	

Item		Standard	Repairing Limit	Remarks
Counter shaft	Radius play	0.01~0.02	0.05 more	
	In. dia.	24.37~24.38 0.959~0.960	24.4 more 0.960	
Bush	In. dia.	17.084~17.134 0.672~0.674	17.2 more 0.677	
	Out. dia.	17.094~17.112 0.672~0.673		
	In. dia.	14.413~14.431 0.567~0.568	14.45 more 0.5689	
Counter shaft & bush	Clearance	0.028~0.04 0.0011~0.0015	0.1 more 0.0039	
Counter shaft & C2 gear	Rotary play	0.01~0.098 0.00039~0.0038	0.5 more 0.0196	
Low gear bush	In. dia.	17.13~17.15 0.674~0.675	17.2 more 0.677	
Low gear bush & 14mm bush	Clearance	0.02~0.058 0.00078~0.0022	0.1 more 0.0039	
Kick starter spindle	Out. dia.	14.341~14.353 0.564~0.565	14.25 less 0.561	
Kick starter spindle & each bush	Clearance	0.06~0.09 0.0023~0.0035	0.15 more 0.0059	
Kick spindle pole	R-part		with step 0.3 more 0.0118	
Kick spindle pole spring	Free length	14 0.5511		
Primary chain	Loosing	5~10 0.1968~0.3937	2.0 less 0.787	

G. Magneto, Contact Point

Item		Standard	Repairing Limit	Remarks
Contact breaker arm spring	Tension	0.2~0.4 0.85~1.05 kg 0.441~0.882 1.874~2.315		In case of 24.5 mm (0.964) of binding length In case of 25.9 mm (1.019) of max. lift
Contact point	Gap	0.3~0.4 0.0118~0.0157	out of standard	
Ignition timing	Crank angle	after upper dead point 5°		
Spark advancer; beginning of advance angle	Rotary number	1100 r.p.m.		
Spark advancer; end of advance angle	Rotary number	3000 r.p.m.	out of standard	

Item		Standard	Repairing Limit	Remarks
Spark advancer; max. advance angle	Crank angle	40°	37°~43°	
Magneto spark character	3 needle gap	8 mm more 0.3149	7 less 0.2755	By kick (500~800 r.p.m.)
Magneto charging character	Charge current	2.0A~3.0A	2A less	At 3000 r.p.m.
Dynamo starter & rotor	Gap	0.5 0.0196	0.8 more 0.0314	Air-gap (in radius)

H. Oil Pump · Oil Separator

Item		Standard	Repairing Limit	Remarks
Oil pump drive gear	Gearing eccentric	0.063 less 0.0039	0.1 more	
Oil pump drive gear & center crank gear	Back lash	0.01 less 0.0039	0.5 more 0.0196	Adjust by packing
Oil pump packing	Thickness	0.4 0.0157		In case of binding
Addendum and internal wall of oil pump gear	Clearance	0.025~0.05	0.1 more 0.0039	
Oil pump gear	Back lash	0.106~0.210 0.0041~0.0082	0.5 more 0.0196	
Side and side cover of oil pump gear	Clearance	0.089~0.04	0.15 more 0.0059	
Gear pin and gear	Clearance	0.05~0.013	0.1 more 0.0039	

I. Kick · R. Crank Case Cover

Item		Standard	Repairing Limit	Remarks
Kick starter joint & hole of crank case cover	Clearance	0.08~0.205	0.5 more 0.0196	
Kick starter spring	Torque	47.6 kgm 344.290 ft lb	40 less 289.32	In case of use

J. Under Crank Case and Change

Item		Standard	Repairing Limit	Remarks
Shift drum	Out. dia.	33.95~33.97 1.336~1.337	33.9 less 1.334	

Item		Standard	Repairing Limit	Remarks
Shift drum & hole of crank case	Out. dia. of axial part	11.966~11.984 0.4711~0.4718	11.9 less 0.4685	
	Clearance	0.025~0.075	0.2 more 0.00787	
Shift drum	Groove width	8.50~8.515 0.334~0.335	9.0 more 0.354	
Shift fork	In. dia. of hole	34.0~34.02 1.338~1.339	34.1 more 1.34	
	Thickness at end	4.9~5.0 0.1929~0.1968	4.5 less 0.177	
Setting stud Bolt of upper, under crank case	Bend at end	0.1 within 0.0039	0.8 more 0.031	
	Torque	0.5~0.7 kgm 3.616~5.063 ftlb	out of standard	D6×P1.0
Stud	Torque	1.7~2.0 kgm 12.29~14.46 ftlb		D8×P1.25

3. FRAME

A. Handle

Item		Standard	Repairing Limit	Remarks
Throttle grip	Play	2~4 0.0787~0.157	out of standard	Check by external periphery
Throttle wire difference between outer & inner	Length	61 2.4015		
Brake lever	Play	25~30 0.984~1.181	out of standard	Check by lever end
Clutch wire ditto	Length	118 4.645		Check by lever end
Clutch lever	Play	15~25 0.590~0.984	out of standard	

B. Front Cushion

Item		Standard	Repairing Limit	Remarks
Front cushion under bush	Out. dia.	26.04~26.07 1.025~1.026	out of standard	
Pivot bush & suspension arm	Clearance	0.037~0.08		
Pivot collar	Overall length	24.5~24.6 0.964~0.968		

Itme		Standard	Repairing Limit	Remarks
Pivot bush & collar	Clearance	0.016~0.07	0.3 more 0.0118	
Front cushion	Stroke	60.3 2.374		
Front cushion damper	Damping force	38~45 kg 83.79~99.22 lb	20 less 44.10	By 0.5 m/sec (19.68 in) of piston
	Oil capacity	39 cc	25 less	White spindle oil #60
Front cushion spring	Free length	278.8 10.976	268 less 10.551	
	Tension	127.5 kg 281.13 lb	110 less 242.55	
	Fall	1° within	out of standard	

C. Front Fork · Steering · Fuel Tank

Item		Standard	Repairing Limit	Remarks
Steering head stem nut	Torque	6.5~7.5 kgm 47.014~54.2 ftlb	out of standard	
Steering head	Angle	90°		Angle between trident and head pipe
Caster		60°		
Trail		75 2.952		
Fuel tank	Capacity	11.8 ℓ 3.115 gal U.S.		

D. Frame Body

Item		Standard	Repairing Lmit	Remarks
Steel ball	Out. dia.	1/4" 0.0098		
Rear fork pivot bolt bush	In. dia.	12.2~12.3 0.480~0.484	12.6 more 0.496	

E. Saddle · Stand

Item		Standard	Repairing Limit	Remarks
Side & main stand spring	Max. tension	38 kg 83.790 lb		
Brake pedal	Food width	20~30 0.787~1.181	out of standard	

F. Rear Fork · Chain Case

Item		Standard	Repairing Limit	Remarks
Rear brake torque link end	Hole	12.1~12.2 0.476~0.480	12.4 more 0.488	
Rear fork pivot bush	Out. dia.	28.0~28.03 1.102~1.103		
Drive chain	Amount of sag	10~20 0.393~0.787	out of standard	95 teeth

G. Rear Cushion

Item		Standard	Repairing Limit	Remarks
Rear cushion	Stroke	61 2.401		
Rear cushion damper	Damping force	50~56 kg 110.25~123.48 lb	30 less 60.15	At 0.5 m/sec (19.68) of piston
	Oil capacity	39 cc	30 less	White spindle oil #60
Rear cushion spring	Free length	218.4~218.9 8.598~8.618	207 less 8.149	
	Tension	150~166 kg 330.75~366.03 lb	143 kg less 315.315 lb	
	Tangential angle	1° within	out of standard	

H. Front Wheel

Item		Standard	Repairing Limit	Remarks
Front wheel hub ball bearing	Axial play	0.005 less	0.1 more 0.00393	
	Radial play	0.01~0.02	0.05 more	

Item		Standard	Repairing Limit	Remarks
Front brake panel spacer	Out. dia.	21.972~21.993 0.8650~0.8658	21.9 less 0.8622	
	Overall length	34.9~35.1 1.374~1.381		
Front axle distance collar	Overall length	49.8~50.2 1.960~1.976		
Brake cam	Thickness	11.9~12.1 0.468~0.476		
Front brake shoe	Out. dia.	174.1~174.4 6.854~6.866		Cutter out. dia.
Front brake lining	Thickness	3.5~4.5 0.137~0.177	2.5 less 0.0984	
Brake drum	In. dia.	174.8~175.2 6.881~6.897	176.0 more 6.929	
Brake shoe spring	Free length	55 2.165	58 more 2.283	
Front axle	Out. dia.	15.0 0.5905	14.9 less 0.586	
Front axle	Bend	0.05 within	0.2 more 0.0078	Both ends support on V block, measure bend at center part
Front wheel rim	Lateral deflection	1.0 within 0.0393	3.0 more 0.118	
Front tire	Air pressure	1.5 kg/cm^2 21.330 lb/in^2	out of standard	

I. Rear Wheel

Item		Standard	Repairing Limit	Remarks
Final driven sprocket	Bottom dia.	145.76 5.738	144.7 less 5.696	
Rear wheel hub bearing	Axial play	0.005 within	0.1 more 0.00393	
	Radial play	0.01~0.02	0.05 more	
Rear axle distance collar	Overall length	73.8~74.2 2.905~2.921		
Rear axle sleeve	Overall length	9.5~9.7 0.374~0.381		
Rear wheel axle	Out. dia.	16.9~17.0 0.665~0.669	16.85 less 0.661	
Rear brake shoe	Bend	0.05 within	0.2 more 0.0078	

Item		Standard	Repairing Limit	Remarks
	Out. dia.	174.1~174.3		Cutter out. dia.
		6.854~6.862		
Rear brake lining	Thickness	3.5~4.5	3.0 less	
		0.137~0.177	0.118	
Rear brake shoe spring	Free length	27.88	32.0 more	
		1.0976	1.259	
Rear brake cam	Thickness	11.9~12.1		
		0.468~0.476		
Rear brake pedal	Foot width	20~30	out of standard	
		0.7874~1.1811		
Rear wheel rim	Lateral deflection	1.0 within	3.0 more	
		0.0393	0.181	
Rear tire	Air pressure	2.0 kg/cm^2	out of standard	
		28.44 lb/in^2		

MEMO

MAINTENANCE STANDARDS, CB72·77

For maintenance operation for HONDA 250·300, Maintenance Standards, specification and dimension are listed hereafter for reference.

EXPLANATION:

Maintenance Items Items to be inspected, service-wise.

Standard Value This indicates the manufacturer's standard size or the standard size after newly assembling or adjusting, and shows the size-limit of completed part in the permissible limit of adjustment.

Repairing Limit Unusable wear limit of parts requiring correction or replacement, function-wise.

Remarks Unmarked numbers are run unit and inch unit shown underneath, and others according to the unit indicated.

UNIT IN CHART:

Unmarked numbers are m/m unit and inch unit shown underneath, and others according to the unit indicated.

CONTENTS

1. GENERAL PERFORMANCE 19

2. ENGINE
   - A. Cylinder, Cylinder Head 19
   - B. Crank Shaft, Connecting Rod, Piston 21
   - C. Cam Shaft, Valve, Cam Chain 24
   - D. Upper, Under Crank Case 26
   - E. Clutch, Crank Case Cover L/H 27
   - F. Transmission 28
   - G. Gear Change 30
   - H. Kick, Crank Case Cover R/H 30
   - I. Oil Pump, Oil Filter 30
   - J. A.C. Dynamo, Starting Motor 32
   - K. Contact Breaker 32

3. FRAME
   - A. Handle 33
   - B. Front Cushion 33
   - C. Steering Stem, Front Fender 35
   - D. Fuel Tank 36
   - E. Frame Body 36
   - F. Stand 37
   - G. Rear Fork, Rear Fender 37
   - H. Rear Cushion 38
   - I. Front Wheel 38
   - J. Rear Wheel 39
   - K. Electric Equipment 40

MAINTENANCE STANDARDS (Model CB72, CB77)

In this list, the dimensions without units indicate "mm" (upper step) and "inch" (down step), and others according to the units indicated. Mark * is exclusively used only for model CB77 and others are common both model CB72 and CB77.

1. GENERAL PERFORMANCE

Item	Standard	Repairing Limit	Adjusting Point	Remarks
Compression pressure	10.5 kg/cm^2 149.34 lb/in^2	8.0kg/cm less 113.78 lb/in^2	Disassemble and adjust	Measure with kick
Fuel Consumption	45 km/ℓ 127 Br m.p.g.	26km/ℓ less 73 Br mpg	Disassemble and adjust	Speed 40km/h (24.8 m.p.h.)
Compression ratio	9.3~9.7	out standard	Disassemble and adjust	
Lubricating oil consumption	120 cc/1000 km less 120 cc/0.62 mile	200cc/1000km more 200cc/0.62 mile	Disassemble and adjust	
Lubricating oil. capacity	1500 cc	out standard	Adjust	Check with oil gauge
Rear wheel output	16PS more * 18PS more	12.5PS less 14PS less	Disassemble and adjust	(Max. output)
Caster	62°	out standard	Exchange	(Referential value)
Trail	85°	out standard	Exchange	(Referential value)

2. ENGINE

A. Cylinder, Cylinder Head

Item		Standard	Repairing Limit	Adjusting Point	Remarks
Cylinder sleeve	Difference between max. in. dia. and min. in. dia.	within 0.01 0.0003	0.05 more 0.00196	Put in boring	After boring, honing should be enforced
Cylinder sleeve	In. dia.	54.00~54.01 2.1259~2.1263 * 60.00~60.01 2.3622~2.3625	54.10 more 2.129 60.10 more 2.366	Put in boring	After boring, honing should be enforced
Cylinder barrel	Height	83.45~93.5 3.285~3.681	out standard		
Cylinder sleeve	Out. dia.	62.02~62.03 2.441~2.442 * 67.02~67.03 2.638~2.6387			(Referential value)

Item		Standard	Repairing Limit	Adjusting Point	Remarks
Cylinder sleeve	Inlaying space	0.02~0.05 0.00078~0.00196			Be pressed in at the normal temperature
Cylinder (oversize)	Over size	0.25 0.0098		Boring	3 category of 0.25
Cylinder head (Cam shaft bearing part)	In. dia.	41.994~42.01 1.653~1.654	42.06 more 1.655	Exchange	
Cylinder head (rocker arm pin)	In. dia.	17.0~17.018 0.669~0.670	17.05 more 0.671	Exchange	
Cylinder head (rocker arm pin)	Combustion chamber capacity	29.3~29.7 cc			(Referential value)
Cylinder head (attaching face)	Bend	0.03 less 0.001	0.06 more 0.002	Rectify	
Cylinder head (head cover attaching face)	Bend	0.03 less 0.001	0.06 more 0.002	Rectify	
Cylinder head (Inlet port)	In. dia.	25.5 1.003			
Carburettor insulator	Gap of the in. dia. of inlet port	0.5 less 0.0196	1.0 more 0.039	Rectify	
Cylinder head gasket	Width	1.0~1.1 0.039~0.043			When tighting
Cylinder packing	Width	0.3~0.4 0.0118~0.0157			When tighting
Tachometer gear	In. dia. of Bush	7.0~7.015 0.275~0.276	7.2 more 0.283	Exchange	
Tachometer gear	Out. dir. of Bush	13.982~14.0 0.550~0.551			
Tachometer gear "O" ring, 14m/m	Tightness	0.4 0.015			Unless omission, there are no troubles
Tachometer gear and bush	Clearance	0.028~0.043 0.001~0.001	0.2 more 0.0078	Exchange	Unless omission, there are no troubles
Cylinder head cover	Flatneess	0.03 less 0.001	0.06 more 0.002	Rectify	
Breather sield plate	Thickness	1.0 0.0393			
Breather sield plate	Attaching direction	put forward an arrow			Be careful of the mark
Cylinder head cover	Tighting torque	1.9~2.3 m-kg 13.73~16.62 ft/ℓb	1.9m-kg less 13.73 ft/ℓb	Rectify	8 spots are equal
Cylinder head cap	Tighting torque	0.45 m-kg 3.25 ft/ℓb	0.35m-kg less 2.53 ft/ℓb	Rectify	
Cylinder head cap "O" ring	Dia.	3.2 0.125	2.5 less 0.0984	Exchange	

B. Crank Shaft, Connecting Rod, Piston

Item		Standard	Repairing Limit	Adjusting Point	Remarks
Crank shaft comp.	Crank angle (I B)	180°			
	Crank angle (II B)	360°			
Sprocket, center crank shaft	Tooth	16			
	Bottom dia.	36.285~36.286 1.428~1.428			
Gear, center crank shaft sprocket	No. of tooth	22			
	Thickness of crossover teeth	15.295~15.337 0.602~0.603	15.1 less 0.594	Exchange	No. of crossover teeth 3
	Out. dia.	47.9~48.0 1.885~1.889	47.7 less 1.877	Exchange	
	Out. dia.	38.003~38.015 1.496~1.496	38.05 more 1.498	Exchange	
	Radial clearance	0.006~0.014	0.05 more	Exchange	
Center crank weight	Out. dia. of pin	25.991~25.999 1.023~1.023	25.95 less 1.021	Exchange	
Center crank shaft, pressed part	In. dia.	25.0~25.02 0.984~0.985	0.00401		(Referential value)
R. crank shaft, bearing part	In. dia.	25.907~25.291 1.019~0.995			
R. crank shaft bearing part	Out. dia.	29.983~29.993 1.180~1.180	29.95 less 1.179	Exchange	
Crank shaft comp.	Max. swing	0.03 less 0.001	0.1 more 0.003	Rectify	
R. Crank shaft key groove	Width	4.0~4.03 0.157~0.158	4.10 more 0.161	Rectify or exchange	
	Thickness	4.0~4.1 0.157~0.161			(Referential value)
	Length	be processed with one cutter			(Referential value)
L. crank shaft pin, pressed part	In. dia.	25.907~25.921 1.019~1.020			
L. crank shaft pressed part	Out. dia.	30.002~30.015 1.181~1.187 * 30.004~30.009 1.181~1.181	25.95 less 1.021 * 29.97 less 1.179	Exchange	
Primary drive sprocket	No. of tooth	15			
	Measuring bottom dia.	39.11~39.21 1.539~1.543	38.9 less 1.531	Exchange	

Item		Standard	Repairing Limit	Adjusting Point	Remarks
Oil filter drive sprocket	No. of tooth	24			
	In. dia.	25.0~25.01 0.984~0.984	26.0 more 1.023	Exchange	
	Measuring bottom dia.	45.15~45.348 1.777~1.785	45.05 less 1.773	Exchange	
Connecting rod small end	In. dia.	15.016~15.043 0.591~0.592	15.1 more 0.594	Exchange	
	Twist	without 0.02 0.0007	0.1 more 0.0039	Exchange	
Connecting rod big end	Thickness	17.97~18.03 0.707~0.709	17.5 less 0.688	Exchange	
	In. dia.	31.005~31.015 1.220~1.221	31.04 more 1.222	Exchange	
	Axial clearance	0.07~0.33 0.002~0.012	0.5 more 0.0196	Exchange	
	Diagonal clearance	0~0.008 0~0.0003	0.05 more 0.0019	Exchange	
Needle roller	Out. dia.	2.502~2.51 0.0985~0.0988	2.5 less 0.098		
	Length	13.45~13.5 0.529~0.531			
	No. reqd.	48 pcs			
Piston pin	Out. dia.	14.994~15.0 0.590~0.5905	14.95 less 0.588	Exchange	
	Overall length	45.9~46.1 1.807~1.814 * 51.9~52.1 2.043~2.051			(Referential value)
Piston head	Dia.	53.65~53.7 2.112~2.114	53.6 less 2.110	Exchange	
		* 59.65~59.7 2.348~2.356	* 59.6 less 2.346	Exchange	
Piston skirt	Dia.	53.98~54.0 2.125~2.126	53.9 less 2.122	Exchange	At the pin boss diagonal direction
		* 59.98~60.0 2.361~2.362	* 59.9 less 2.358	Exchange	
Piston	Taper	First step D- 0.06~0.07 D-0.002~0.002	out-standard	Exchange	
		Second step D- 0.12~0.14 D-0.004~0.005			Measure at the pin boss diagonal direction
	Ellipse	0.14~0.16 0.005~0.006	out-standard	Exchange	Measure at 5 m/m upper point from the foot of skirt

Item		Standard	Repairing Limit	Adjusting Point	Remarks
Piston ring groove (Top)	Groove width	1.505~1.52 0.0593~0.0598	1.55 more 0.061	Exchange	
Piston ring groove (Second)	Groove width	1.505~1.52 0.0593~0.0598	1.55 more 0.061	Exchange	
Piston ring groove (Oil)	Groove width	2.805~2.82 0.011~0.0111	2.95 more 0.0116		
Piston ring groove	Out. dia.	48.1~48.2 1.893~1.897 * 53.3~53.4 2.098~2.102	47.9 less 1.885 * 53.1 less 2.090	Exchange Exchange	
Piston & cylinder	Min. clearance		0.06 more 0.0023	Exchange	
Piston oversize	Oversize	0.25 0.0098		Exchange	3 category of 0.25 (0.0098) oversize
Piston ring (Top)	Width	1.45~1.46 0.057~0.0574 * 1.45~1.465 0.057~0.0576	1.4 less 0.0551 * 1.4 less * 0.0551	Exchange Exchange	
Piston ring (Second)	Thickness	2.4~2.6 0.0944~0.102 * 2.6~2.8 0.0944~0.110	2.2 less 0.0866 * 2.4 less 0.0944	Exchange Exchange	
Piston ring (Top)	Tension	0.62~0.82 kg 1.366~1.807 lbs * 0.7~1.0 kg 1.543~2.204 lbs	0.5 kg less 1.102 lbs * 0.6 kg less 1.322 lbs	Exchange Exchange	Tangential tension
	End gap	0.15~0.35 0.0059~0.013 * 0.2~0.4 0.0078~0.0157	0.6 more 0.023 * 0.65 more 0.0255	Rectify the narrow ring Exchange the wide ring	When attaching
Piston ring (Second)	Width	1.48~1.495 0.0582~0.0588	1.43 less 0.0562	Exchange	
	Thickness	2.4~2.6 0.0944~0.102 * 2.6~2.8 0.0944~0.110	2.2 less 0.0866 * 2.4 less 0.0944	Exchange Exchange	
	Tension	0.6~0.8 kg 1.322~1.763 lbs * 0.7~1.0 kg 1.543~2.204 lbs	0.5 kg less 1.102 lbs * 0.6 kg less 1.322 lbs	Exchange Exchange	Tangential tension
	End gap	0.15~0.35 0.0059~0.013 * 0.2~0.4 0.0078~0.0157	0.6 more 0.023 * 0.65 more 0.0255	Rectify the narrow ring Exchange the wide ring	When attaching

Item		Standard	Repairing Limit	Adjusting Point	Remarks
Piston ring (Oil)	Width	2.4~2.6 0.0944~0.102	2.0 less (0.0787)	Exchange	
		* 2.78~2.795 0.109~0.110		Exchange	
	Thickness	2.78~2.795 0.109~0.110	2.7 less 0.106	Exchange	
		* 2.6~2.8 0.0944~0.110	* 2.5 less 0.0984	Exchange	
	Tension	0.7~0.9 kg 1.543~1.984 lbs	0.5 kg less 1.102 lbs	Exchange	Tangential tension
		* 0.9~1.15 kg 1.984~2.53 lbs	0.7 kg less 1.543 lbs	Exchange	
	End gap	0.1~0.3 0.00393~0.0118	0.8 more 0.0314	Rectify the narrow ring Exchange the wide ring	When attaching
Piston ring & groove (Top)	Clearance	0.045~0.07	0.15 more 0.0059	Exchange	
		* 0.04~0.07	* 0.15 more * 0.0059	Exchange	
Piston ring & groove (Second)	Clearance	0.01~0.04	0.1 more 0.00393	Exchange	
Piston ring & groove (Oil)	Clearance	0.01~0.04	0.1 more 0.00393	Exchange	
Piston ring oversize	Oversize	0.25 0.00984			3 category of 0.25 oversize

C. Cam Shaft Valve Cam Chain

Item		Standard	Repairing Limit	Adjusting point	Remarks
Cam shaft (Bearing part)	Out. dia.	19.996~20.009 0.787~0.787	19.95 less 0.785	Exchange	
Cam (Bearing part)	Height	In 31.67~31.71 1.246~1.248	31.4 1.236	Exchange	
		Ex. 30.54~30.58 1.202~1.203	30.2 less 1.188		
Cam shaft	Lift	In 5.69 0.118 Ex. 4.56 0.179			Max. lift
Cam sprocket complete	Nos. of teeth	32			
	Bottom dia.	74.766 2.943	74.2 less 2.921	Exchange	

Item		Standard	Repairing Limit	Adjusting point	Remarks
Cam chain	Type	DK-219			
	Length	723.0~723.8	728.0	Exchange	
		28.464~28.496	28.661 more		
Exhaust valve	Thickness	1.0	0.5 less		
		0.0393	0.00196		
Exhaust valve (Stem)	Out. dia.	6.96~6.97	6.94 less	Rectify or	
		0.274~0.274	0.273	Exchange	
Exhaust valve (Seat face)	Angle	90~91°	out-standard	Exchange	
Exhaust valve	Overall length	88.74~88.76	89.4 less	Exchange	
		3.493~3.494	3.519		
Inlet valve	Thickness	1.0	0.5 less	Exchange	
		0.039	0.019		
Inlet valve (Stem)	Out. dia.	6.98~6.99	6.96 less	Exchange	
		0.274~0.275	0.274	or rectify	
Inlet valve (Seat)	Angle	90°~91°	out-standard	Exchange	
Inlet valve	Overall length	89.96~89.98	89.6 less	Exchange	
		3.541~3.542	3.521		
Valve spring (Inner)	Free length	37.54	36.0 less	Exchange	
		1.477	1.417		
	Diagonal degree	0.8 less	1.5 more	Exchange	
	Tension	7.6~8.4 kg	60 kg less	Exchange	
		18.9~20.1 kg	16.0 kg less		
		16.754~18.518	13.227		
		41.667~44.313	35.273		
Valve spring (Outer)	Free length	43.36	42.0 less	Exchange	
		1.707	1.653		
	Diagonal degree	0.8 less	1.5 more	Exchange	
	Tension	16.9~18.1 kg	15.0 kg less	Exchange	
		34.4~34.6 kg	32.0 kg less		
		37.257~29.903 lbs	33.069 lbs less		
		75.838~76.279 lbs	70.547 lbs less		
Exhaust valve guide	In. dia.	7.0~7.01	7.05 more	Exchange	
		0.275~0.2759	0.2775		
Inlet valve guide	In. dia.	7.0~7.01	7.05 more	Exchange	
		0.275~0.2759	0.2775		
Valve seat	Touch width	1.0	20 more	Rectify	Repair of cylinder head
		0.039	0.08		
Rocker arm	In. dia.	13.0~13.027	13.1 more	Exchange	
		0.511~0.512	0.515		
Rocker arm shaft (Rocker arm part)	Out. dia.	12.966~12.984	12.9 less	Exchange	
		0.510~0.511	0.507		

Item		Standard	Repairing Limit	Adjusting point	Remarks
Rocker arm shaft (Inlay part of head)	Out. dia.	16.994~16.976 0.669~0.668	16.95 less 0.667	Exchange	
Rocker arm shaft (Oil port)	In. dia.	2.5 0.0984			
Tappet clearance	In. Ex.	0.08~0.12 0.003~0.047	out-standard	Rectify	Cold type
Cam chain tensioner roller	Out. dia.	40 1.574	38 less 1.496	Exchange	Aging and crack of rubber should not be.
Cam chain tensioner roller (Spring)	Free length	63.3 2.492	60.0 less 2.362	Exchange	
	Tension	7 kg 15.432 lbs	5.5 kg less 12.125 lbs	Exchange	Referential value-control by over all length
Valve timing ex.	Opening angle	before lower dead point 35°	out-standard ±5°	Rectify	Check at 1.1 m/m (In case of lift)
	Closing angle	after upper dead point 10°	out-standard ±5°	Rectify	Check at 1.1 m/m (In case of lift)
Valve timing In.	Opening angle	before upper dead point 5°	out-standard ±5°	Rectify	Check at 1.1 m/m (In case of lift)
	Closing angle	after lower dead point 30°	out-standard ±5°	Rectify	Check at 1.1 m/m (In case of lift)

D. Upper · Under Crank Case

Item		Standard	Repairing Limit	Adjusting point	Remarks
Upper·under crank case (Part of center bearing)	In. dia.	65.97~65.987 2.597~2.598	66.04 more 2.60	Exchange	Combined with upper and under and then measure
Upper·under crank case (Part of bearing L/H, R/H)	In. dia.	L/H 76.97~76.987 R/H 64.97~64.987 3.0307~3.0309 2.557~2.558	76.93 more 64.93 more 3.0287 2.556	Exchange	Combined with upper and under and then measure
Upper·under crank case (Part of mission shaft)	In. dia.	61.985~61.996 2.440~2.4407	62.04 more 2.442	Exchange	Combined with upper and under and then measure
Upper·under crank case (Part of kick spindle)	In. dia.	25.0~25.021 0.984~0.985	25.1 more 0.988	Exchange Rectify	Combined with upper and under and then measure
Upper·under crank case (Seam surface)	Flatness	within 0.03 0.001	0.06 more 0.002	Rectify	
Cylinder attaching face of upper crank case	Flatness	within 0.03 0.001	0.06 more 0.002	Rectify	

Item		Standard	Repairing Limit	Adjusting point	Remarks
L/H cover attaching face of upper crank case	Flatness	within 0.03 0.001	0.06 more 0.002	Rectify	
Cam chain guide roller	Out. dia.	59.5 2.342	58.0 less 2.28	Exchanga	Aging and crack of rubber should not remain
	In. dia.	14.0~14.018 0.551~0.5518	14.1 more 0.555	Exchange	
Cam chain guide roller pin	Out. dia.	13.966~13.984 0.549~0.550	13.9 less 0.547	Exchange	
Oil level gauge "O" ring 22 mm	Dia.	2.9~3.1 0.114~1.22	2.8 less 0.110	Exchange	
	Tightness	2.0 0.078	0.5 less 0.0019	Exchange	
Under crank case attaching face of cover L/H	Flatness	within 0.03 0.001	0.06 more 0.002	Rectify	
Under crank case (Seam surface of upper·under)	Flatness	within 0.03 0.0012	0.06 more 0.0023	Rectify	
Under crank case seam surface	Slip out of L/H or R/H	within 0.05 0.00019	0.1 more 0.0039	Rectify	

E. Clutch. Crank Case Cover L/H

Item		Standard	Repairing Limit	Adjusting point	Remarks
Clutch friction disc	Thickness	2.9~3.0 0.114~1.181	2.5 less 0.984	Exchange	One set is 6 sheets
	In. dia.	112 4.409			
	Flatness	within 0.2 0.0078	0.4 more 0.015	Exchange	
Clutch plate	Thickness	2.0 0.078	1.6 less 0.0629	Exchange	Use 5 sheets
	Flatness	within 0.2 0.0078	0.4 more 0.015	Exchange or Repairing	
	Out. dia.	135 5.314			
Clutch center and clutch plate	Clearance of rotary direction	within 0.3 0.0118	0.3 more 0.0118	Exchange	Clearance at out. dia. of plate
Clutch center and mission shaft	Clearance of rotary direction	within 0.1 0.0039	0.3 more 0.0118	Exchange	

Item		Standard	Repairing Limit	Adjusting point	Remarks
Clutch outer comp. (with sprocket)	Teeth	47 (1.85)			
	Bottom dia.	136.15~136.16 5.360~5.3606	135.5 less 5.334	Exchange	Measure bottom dia., roller dia. 0.35 Referential value
	In. dia.	88.0~88.035 3.464~3.465			
Clutch center and mission shaft	Axial clearance	0.027~0.067 0.001~0.0026	0.2 more 0.0078 more	Exchange	
Clutch pressure plate	Flatness	within 0.1 0.0039	0.3 more 0.0118	Exchange	
	In. dia.	112 (4.409)			
Clutch spring	Free length	33.4 1.314	32.4 less 1.275	Exchange	
	Diagonal degree	1.0 less 0.0393	2.0 more 0.0787	Exchange	
	Load	15.3~15.7 kg 33.73~34.61 lbs	13.6 kg less 29.982 lbs	Exchange	
Crank case cover L/H	Flatness	within 0.01 0.0003	0.06 more 0.0023	Rectify	
Crank case cover L/H (Part of oil filter)	In. dia.	58.0~58.046 2.283~2.285			
Crank case cover L/H ("O" ring)	Tightness	0.5 more 0.0197	out-standard	Exchange	
Crank case cover L/H (Part of shift spindle)	In. dia.	14.0~14.018 0.551~0.5518	14.1 more 0.555	Exchange	
Crank case cover L/H (Packing)	Thickness	0.3~0.4 0.0118~0.0157			When disassembly and maintenance, exchange should be done each time.

F. Transmission

Item		Standard	Repairing Limit	Adjusting point	Remarks
Transmission	Type	Four speed Constant mesh gear			
Main shaft	Out. dia.	24.959~24.98 0.968~0.983	24.9 less 0.980	Exchange	
Main shaft and M_2 gear	Clearance	0.02~0.074 0.007~0.00291	0.1 more 0.0039	Exchange	
Main shaft	Axial Clearance	0.1~0.75 0.0039~0.0295	1.2 more 0.0472	Exchange	

Item		Standard	Repairing Limit	Adjusting point	Remarks
Main shaft and M₃ gear	Clearance of rotary direction	0.03~0.078 0.0012~0.00307	0.1 more 0.0039	Exchange	
Mission gear	Back rush	0.089~0.178 0.0035~0.0070	0.2 more 0.0078	Exchange	
Top gear	In. dia.	18.0~18.018 0.708~0.709	18.2 more 0.716	Exchange	
Top gear (lifter rod part)	In. dia.	8.0~8.015 0.314~0.315	8.06 more 0.317	Exchange	
Top gear (Bush)	In. dia.	20.5~20.521 0.807~0.8079	20.6 more 0.811	Exchange	
Top gear bush and mission shaft	Clearance	0.081 0.00318	0.1 more 0.0039	Exchange	(Part of 20.5ø)
Drive sprocket	Bottom dia.	65.649~65.776 2.584~2.589	64.7 less 2.547	Exchange	
Drive sprocket (Rotary direction)	Clearance	0.03~0.078 0.00118~0.00307	0.25 more 0.0984	Exchange	
Counter shaft (gear side)	In. dia.	24.37~24.385 0.959~0.960	24.4 more 0.9606	Exchange	
Counter shaft	Out. dia.	24.96~24.939 0.982~0.981	24.9 less 0.980	Exchange	
Bush 14 mm	In. dia.	14.375~14.393 0.565~0.566	15.2 more 0.598	Exchange	
	Out. dia.	24.98~25.013 0.983~0.984		Exchange	
Counter shaft and C₂ gear	Clearance of rotary direction	0.01~0.098 0.00039~0.0038	0.2 more 0.0078	Exchange	
Low gear	Crossover thickness	21.667~21.714 0.853~0.854	21.6 less 0.850	Exchange	
Kick startor spindle and bush 14 mm	Clearance	0.022~0.052 0.0087~0.00204	0.15 more 0.0059	Exchange	
Bush C 14 mm	Out. dia.	17.094~17.112 0.672~0.673	17.05 less 0.671	Exchange	
	In. dia.	14.413~14.431 0.567~0.568	14.53 more 0.572	Exchange	
Mission gear gear ratio	First	3.12			
	2nd	1.74			
	3rd	1.27			
	Top	1.00			
Kick spindle pole spring	Free length	14 0.551	13.5 less 0.531	Exchange	

Item		Standard	Repairing Limit	Adjusting point	Remarks
Kick spindle pole bush pin	Out. dia.	5 0.196	4.5 less 0.177	Exchange	
	Overall length	13 0.511	12.5 less 0.492	Exchange	
Primary chain	Deflection	5~10 0.196~0.393	20 more 0.7874	Exchange	Show by max. swing of loosing
Roller 5×6.25	No. Reqd.	12 pieces			

G. Gear Change

Item		Standard	Repairing Limit	Adjusting point	Remarks
Gear shift fork	In. dia.	34.0~34.025 1.338~1.339	34.2 more 1.346	Exchange	
Gear shift drum	Out. dia.	33.95~33.975 1.336~1.337	33.9 less 1.334	Exchange	
Drum and shift fork	Clearance	0.025~0.075 0.0098~0.0295	0.25 more 0.0098	Exchange	
Gear change pedal	In. dia.	17.0~17.027 0.669~0.670	17.3 more 0.709	Exchange	

H. Kick, Crank Case Cover R/H

Item		Standard	Repairing Limit	Adjusting point	Remarks
Kick startor gear	Shaft Out. dia.	14.341~14.353 0.564~0.565	14.25 less 0.561	Exchange	
Kick startor gear and cover R/H	Clearance	0.016~0.104 0.00063~0.0409	0.3 more 0.0118	Exchange	
Cover R/H	Flatness	within 0.05 0.000196	0.1 more 0.0039	Rectify or exchange	

I. Oil Pump, Oil Filter

Item		Standard	Repairing Limit	Adjusting point	Remarks
Oil pump drive gear	Teeth width	4 0.157			
	Bend	0.05 0.00019	0.1 more 0.00393	Exchange	
Oil pump drive gear and M. crank gear	Back rush	0.085~0.127 0.00334~0.050	0.15 more 0.059	Rectify	Adjust by packing
Oil pump gear top and inside wall	Clearance	0.025~0.05 0.0098~0.0019	0.1 more 0.00393	Exchange	

Item		Standard	Repairing Limit	Adjusting point	Remarks
Oil pump gear	Back rush	0.106~0.21 0.00417~0.0082	0.4 more 0.015	Exchange	
Oil pump gear side face and side cover	Clearance	0.04~0.089 0.0015~0.0035	0.1 more 0.0039	Exchange	
Oil pump gear and pin	Clearance	0.013~0.05 0.00511~0.00019	0.3 more 0.00118	Exchange	
Oil filter shaft and oil filter rotor	Clearance	0.012~0.048 0.00472~0.00188	0.1 more 0.0039	Exchange	
Oil filter rotor	Out. dia.	57 2.244			
Oil filter chain	Loosing	5~10 0.196~3.937	15 more 5.905	Exchange	Measure the amplitude at the center

J. A. C Dynamo Starting Motor

Item		Standard	Repairing Limit	Adjusting point	Remarks
Spark performance on ignition	3 Needle gap	8 more 300 r.p.m. 0.314	7 less 0.275	Exchange	3 Needle gap
Charging performance on dynamo	Charging current	2.0~3.0A	out-standard	Exchange	start of charging, at 1700 r.p.m., after that, at 500 r.p.m.
Dynamo starter and rotor	Clearance	0.5 0.0197	0.8 more 0.0314	Exchange	
Starting clutch outer and dynamo	Out. dia. gap	0~0.06 0~0.00236	0.1 more 0.0039	Exchange	
Cross screw 6×24	Tighting torque	0.5 m-kg 3.615 ft/lb	out-standard	Rectify	When tighting, screw rock should be needed.
Clutch roller spring	Free length	25~31 0.984~1.220	24 less 0.944	Exchange	
Clutch roller spring (Cap)	In. dia.	4.1~4.25 0.161~0.167	4.3 more 0.169	Exchange	
	Out. dia.	5.2~5.3 0.2047~0.2086	5.0 less 0.196	Exchange	
Starting sprocket of clutch outer journal	Out. dia.	37.175~37.2 1.463~1.464	37.1 less 1.460	Exchange	
Starting motor	Voltage	12 V			
	Horse power	0.4 KW	out-standard	Exchange	
	Rating	30 sec	out-standard	Exchange	

K. Contact breaker

Item		Standard	Repairing Limit	Adjusting point	Remarks
Contact point	Max. gap	0.35 0.01377	out-standard	Repairing	
Ignition timing	Crank angle	before upper dead point 5°	3° less 7° more	Repairing	
Spark advancer advanced beginning	R.P.M.	1100 r.p.m. (5°)	out-standard	Exchange	
Spark advancer advanced finish	R.P.M.	3300 r.p.m. (45°)	out-standard	Exchange	
Spark advancer advanced max. advanced angle	Crank angle	40°	37°~43° out-range	Exchange	

L. Carburettor

Item		Standard	Repairing Limit	Adjusting point	Remarks
Carburettor	Type	PW 22H ^R_L A4a * PW 26			
	Main jet	# 100 * # 135			
	Air jet	# 150			
	Air bleed	A B 1 1.0ø × 2 * 1.8ø × 4 A B 2 0.7ø × 2 * 0.8ø × 2 A B 3 0.7ø × 4 * 0.7ø × 2			
	Needle jet	2.6 ø			
	Jet needle	22402-2 step * 24231-3 step			
	Cutter way	# 3 width 1.2 cutting depth 0.5 * # 2 nothing			
	Air screw	1~1½ return * 1¼ return			
	Slow jet	# 35 (0.8ø × 4 pieces × 2 step) * # 42 (0.8ø × 2 pieces × 4 step)			

Item		Standard	Repairing Limit	Adjusting point	Remarks
Carburettor	Valve seat	2.5⌀ * 2.0⌀			
	Pilot outlet	1.2⌀			
	Power jet	# 160			
	Power air jet	# 90			

3. FRAME BLOCK
A. Handle

Item		Standard	Repairing Limit	Adjusting point	Remarks
Circumference direction of throttle grip	Play	4~8 0.157~0.314	out-standard	Rectify	Measure at out circumference
Difference between outer and inner of throttle wire	Length	55 2.165	out-standard	Rectify or exchange	
Clutch wire difference between outer & inner	Length	133 5.236	out-standard	Rectify or exchange	
Brake lever	Play	25~30 0.984~1.417	out-standard	Rectify	Check by lever end
Clutch lever	Play	15~25 0.590~0.984	out-standard	Rectify	
Front fork cover cushion	Thickness	6.5 0.0255	6.0 less 0.0236	Exchange	
	Out. dia.	39 1.535			

B. Front Cushion

Item		Standard	Repairing Limit	Adjusting ponit	Remarks
Front cushion	Type	Telescope type	out-standard	Rectify or exchange	
	Stroke	80 3.149	out-standard		
	Oil capacity	both of R. and L. 250 cc	out-standard		
Front cushion spring	Free length (One step)	185.5 7.303	180 less 7.08	Exchange	Reference value

Item		Standard	Repairing Limit	Adjusting point	Remarks
Front cushion spring	Free length (Two step)	221.5 8.720	216.5 less 8.523	Exchange	Reference value
	Overall length	407.0 16.024	396.0 less 15.590	Exchange	
	Available winding Nos. (First step)	32			
	Available winding Nos. (Secondary step)	30			Reference value
	Height in case of bind	374 14.724			Reference value
	Torque in case of bind	24.1 kg 53.13 lbs			Reference value
	Overall winding Nos.	62	out-standard	Exchange	
	Dia. of coil	4.5 0.177			Reference value
	Coil out. dia.	25.0~25.5 0.984~1.004			
Front fork pipe comp.	Bend	within 0.1 0.0039	0.15 more 0.0059	Exchange	The bend of pipe nut, when made the plating part a fulcrum
Front fork pipe piston	Out. dia.	37.45~37.475 1.474~1.475	37.4 less 1.472	Exchange	
Front fork valve	In. dia.	32.98~33.019 1.298~1.299	33.1 more 1.303	Exchange	
Front fork pipe piston valve	Space between fork pipe	0.055~0.109 0.0021~0.0042	0.2 more 0.0078		
	Foot face flat degree	0.02 0.00078	out-standard	Rectify or change	Roughness should be 1.5S more
Front fork bottom case	In. dia.	37.5~37.539 1.476~1.4779	37.65 more 1.482	Change	
	Out. dia.	41.236~41.275 1.623~1.625	41.15 1.620 less	Change	
Front fork bottom piece axis part (R)	In. dia.	15.0~15.043 0.590~0.592	15.1 more 0.594	Change	
Front fork bottom piece axis part (L)	In. dia.	20.0~20.52 0.7874~0.807	20.2 more 0.795	Change	
Seal housing bottom case inlaying space	In. dia.	41.3~41.362 1.625~1.628	41.5 more 1.633	Change	

Item		Standard	Repairing Limit	Adjusting point	Remarks
Seal housing & oil seal	In. dia.	46.0~46.039 1.811~1.812	out-standard		
	Inlaying space	0.06~0.3 0.0023~0.011			
Fork pipe guide	Overall length	36 1.417	out-standard	Change	
	In. dia.	33.0~33.039 1.299~1.300	33.1 more 1.303		
	Out. dia.	37.466~37.491 1.475~1.476	out-standard	Exchange	
Front fork upper	Overall length	173.8~174.2 6.842~6.858	out-standard	Exchange	
Front fork upper (Upper part)	Out. dia.	42 1.654			
Front fork upper (Cover cushion inlaying part)	Out. dia.	34.4~34.6 1.354~1.362	out-standard	Exchange	
	In. dia.	33.2~33.4 1.307~1.314	out-standard	Exchange	
Front fork under cover	Overall length	175 6.889			
Front fork under cover (Upper part)	Out. dia.	54 2.125			
	In. dia.	38.5 1.515			
Fork rib upper cover inlaying part	In. dia.	54.5~54.7 2.145~2.153	out-standard	Exchange	
Fork rib under cover inlaying part	Out. dia.	55 2.165			
	In. dia.	38.1~38.3 1.500~1.507			

C. Steering Stem, Front Fender

Item		Standard	Repairing Limit	Adjusting point	Remarks
Stem & bottom cone race	Binding space	0.007~0.041	0.004 less	Exchange	
Steering head stem nut	Binding torque	6.5~7.5 m-kg 46.99~54.22 ft/lb	5 m-kg less 36.15 ft/lb	Rectify	
Steering stem top cone race inlaying part	Out. dia.	25.979~26.0 1.022~1.023			
Steering stem front fork pipe inlaying part	In. dia.	38.0~38.062 1.496~1.498	38.25 more 1.505	Exchange	

Item		Standard	Repairing Limit	Adjusting point	Remarks
Steering stem bottom bridge	Stopper angle	76° (double, side ±5 mm)	out-standard	Rectify or exchange	Measured by jig (referential value)
Steering top cone race	In. dia.	26.0~26.021 1.023~1.024	out-standard	Exchange	
Front fender	Plank	0.8 0.031			
	Material	SPC-1			

D. Fuel Tank

Item		Standard	Repairing Limit	Adjusting point	Remarks
Fuel tank	Volume	14 ℓ			
	Reserve	1.2~1.5 ℓ			

E. Frame Body

Item		Standard	Repairing Limit	Adjusting point	Remarks
Head pipe comp. top ball race	Binding space	0.051~0.0575 0.002~0.0022	out-standard	Rectify or exchange	
Head pipe comp. bottom race		0.001~0.051	out-standard	Rectify or exchange	
Steel ball	Out. dia.	¼″ 0.009			
Steel ball top	No. Reqd.	18 pcs	out-standard	Rectify or exchange	
Steel ball bottom	No. Reqd.	19 pcs	out-standard	Rectify or exchange	
Rear fork center bush	In. dia.	14.01~14.02 0.551~0.551	14.1 more 0.555	Exchange	
	Binding space	0.03~0.08 0.001~0.003			

F. Stand

Item		Standard	Pepairing Limit	Adjusting point	Remarks
Step arm comp.	In. dia.	12.2 0.480	12.7 more 0.499	Exchange	
Step arm fixing bolt	Out. dia.	16.957~16.984 0.667~0.668	16.7 less 0.657	Exchange	
Main stand pipe	Thickness	2.3 0.090			
Main stand the hole of binding part	In. dia.	14.0~14.027 0.551~0.552	14.3 more 0.562	Exchange	
Main stand setting bolt	Out. dia.	13.9~13.968 0.547~0.549	13.5 less 0.531	Exchange	
Main stand setting spring	Free length	86 3.385	83 less 3.26	Exchange	
	Load	87.5 kg 192.902 lbs	86.2 kg less 190.003 lbs	Exchange	In case of binding, max. stretch and load (referential value)
Brake pedal	In. dia.	17.0~17.027 0.669~0.670	17.2 more 0.677	Exchange	
	Clearance	20~30 0.787~1.18	out-standard	Rectify	

G. Rear Fork, Rear Fender

Item		Standard	Pepairing Limit	Adjusting point	Remarks
Rear fork pivot	In. dia.	26.0~26.021 1.023~1.024			
Rear fork pivot bush	Out. dia.	26.04~26.08 1.025~1.026		Exchange	After pressed in give a finishing touch to the in. dia.
	In. dia.	20.05~20.08 0.789~0.790	20.5 more 0.807	Exchange	
	Pressed space	0.019~0.08 0.0007~0.003	Clearance	Exchange	
Rear fork pivot bolt	Out. dia.	13.925~13.968 0.548~0.549	13.8 less 0.543		
Drive chain	Overall length	301 11.850			
	Type	DK 530			
	Teeth	94 teeth			
	Slack	9~13 0.354~0.511	out-standard	Rectify or exchange	

Item		Standard	Pepairing Limit	Adjusting point	Remarks
Rear brake stopper arm	In. dia.	10.1~10.2 0.397~0.401	10.7 more	Exchange	
	Thickness	9 0.354	out-standard	Exchange	
	Overall length	385 15.157			

H. Rear Cushion

Item		Standard	Pepairing Limit	Adjusting point	Remarks
Rear cushion	Stroke	60 2.362	out-standard	Rectify or exchange	
	Oil capacity	52 cc	out-standard	Rectify	#60 spindle oil
	Declined tension	60~67 kg/0.5 m/s 132.27~147.70 lbs/0.5 m/s	out-standard	Exchange	
Rear cushion spring	Free length	210 8.267	207 less 8.149	Exchange	In case of 185 mm (binding height)
	Load	37.5 kg 82.672 lbs	33 kg less 72.75 lbs	Exchange	

I. Front Wheel

Item		Standard	Pepa'ring Limit	Adjusting point	Remarks
Front axle disrance collar	Overall length	49.9~50.1 1.964~1.972		Exchange	
Front brake cam	Thickness	10 0.393	8 less 0.314	Exchange	
Front brake shoe	Out. dia.	199.8~200 7.866~7.874			Shave out. dia.
Front brake lining	Thickness	5 0.196	2.5 less 0.098	Exchange	
Brake drum	In. dia.	199.85~200.15 7.868~7.879	201 more 7.913	Exchange	
Brake shoe spring	Free length	63.0~63.5 2.480~2.499	66.5 more 2.618	Exchange	
	Load	5 kg 11.023 lbs	3.5 kg less 7.716 lbs	Exchange	In case of 67.5mm (setting length)
Front axle	Out. dia.	14.966~14.984 0.589~0.589	14.9 less 0.586	Exchange	

Item		Standard	Pepairing Limit	Adjusting point	Remarks
Front Axle	Out. dia.	19.008~19.96 0.748~0.785	19.9 less 0.783	Exchange	
	Overall length	238 9.370			
	Bend	0.05 0.00019	0.2 more 0.007	Rectify or exchange	
Front wheel rim	Swing	1.0 0.0393	3.0 more 0.118	Rectify or exchange	
Front tire	Dimension	2.75~18 0.108~0.708			4PR
	Air pressure	1.7 kg/cm² 24.179 lb/in²	out-standard	Rectify	
Front panel axle	In. dia.	15.0~15.018 0.590~0.591	15.1 more 0.594	Exchange	

J. Rear Wheel

Item		Standard	Pepairing Limit	Adjusting point	Remarks
Final driven sprocket	Bottom dia.	151.8 5.975	150.8 less 5.936	Exchange	
Rear axle distance collar	Overall length	100~100.2 3.937~3.944	out-standard	Exchange	
Rear wheel axle	Out. dia.	19.947~19.98 0.785~0.786	19.8 less 0.779	Exchange	
	Bend	0.05	0.2 more	Rectify or exchange	
	Overall length	280 11.023			
Rear brake shoe	Out. dia.	199.8~200 7.866~7.874			Shave out. dia.
Rear brake lining	Thickness	5 0.196	2.5 less 0.0984	Exchange	
Rear wheel rim	Swing	1.0 0.0393	3.0 more 0.118	Rectify or exchange	
Rear wheel tire	Air pressure	2.2 kg/cm² 31.290 lb/in²		Rectify	
	Dimension	3.00~18 0.118~0.708			4PR
Rear brake panel axle	In. dia.	20.0~20.033 0.787~0.788	20.1 0.791	Exchange	
Rear brake panel torque	In. dia.	10.1~10.2 0.397~0.401	10.5 0.41	Exchange	
Brake cam	In. dia.	15.0~15.043 0.590~0.592	15.3 0.602	Exchange	

K. Electric Equipments

Item		Standard	Pepairing Limit	Adjusting point	Remarks
Head light bulb	Electric current	35/30W 2.67A			12V
Stop lamp	Electric current	7.5W 0.58A			
Tail lamp	Electric current	4W 0.28A			
Serenium rectifire	Output volt	DC 30V			
	Input power	AC 40V			
Phon	Phon	95~105 phon	95 phon less	Adjust or exchange	Adjust by screw
Fuse	Capacity	15A			
Battery	Electrolyte capacity	0.7 ℓ	out-standard	Adjust the liquid level	
	Capacity	10AH			
	Volt	12V	when 1A is charging, 10.6V less	Charge	
	Specific gravity of electrolyte	1.260~1.280	1.18 less	Adjust	
Stop switch	Max. ampere	PC 2A			
	Stroke	6~8			
Combination switch	Max. ampere	6 A			
	Max. ampere	4 A			
	Insulation Resistance	50MΩ 10MΩ	1MΩ less 0.1MΩ less	Exchange Exchange	
Speedometer	Error	−0+5%	out-standard	Exchange	
Tachometer	4000 r.p.m. less	±200 r.p.m.	out-standard	Rectify or exchange	
	4000~6000	±235	out-standard	Exchange	
	6000~8000	±270	out-standard	Exchange	
	8000~10000	±300	out-standard	Exchange	
	10000~12000	±400	out-standard	Exchange	

DISASSEMBLY AND ASSEMBLY

In this chapter, mainly Disassembly operation was explained, and for assembly special attention was only called for where needed, as both operation are similar.

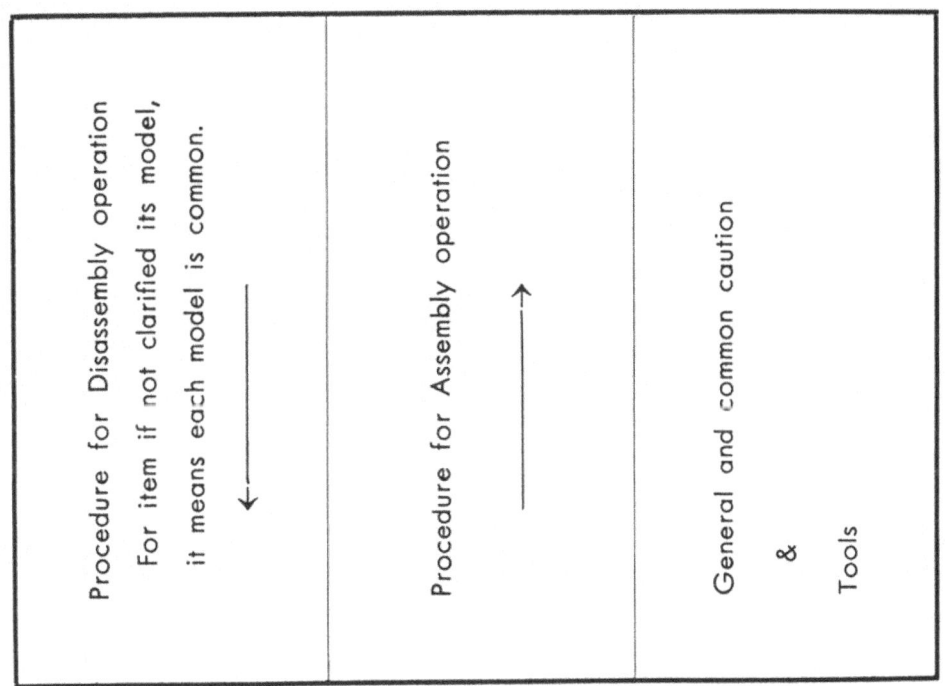

CONTENTS

1. ENGINE (C72 · 77)

    A. Engine replacement 45

    B. Cylinder.. 51

    C. L. Cover 56

    D. R. Cover 60

    E. Mission (Crank).. 62

    F. Cylinder Head 64

    G. Oil Pump 68

2. ENGINE (CB72 · 77)

    A. Engine Replacement 70

    B. Cylinder 76

    C. Engine Minor Overhaul, Assembly 77

3. FRAME (CB72 · 77)

    A. Rear Fork 78

    B. Front Fork 81

DISASSEMBLY AND ASSEMBLY

1. ENGINE (C72 · 77)

A. Engine Replacement (L. side)

Disassembly	Assembly	Precaution Tools	
1. L. Exhaust pipe joint nut	Tighten not to leak exhaust gas.	10 m/m socket wrench	Fig. 1
2. L. Exhaust pipe muffler		14 m/m socket wrench 17 m/m spanner	Fig. 2
3. L. step bar	Be cautious of the position of seration in case of fitting. Assemble with putting in position at the punch mark. Tightening torque 2.1kgm (15ft. lb)	14 m/m spanner	Fig. 3
4. Gear change pedal	Fitting angle, one seration foreward inclined from horizontal position.	10 m/m spanner	Fig. 4

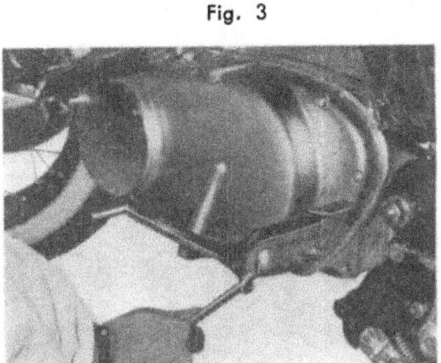

	Disassembly	Assembly	Precaution Tools

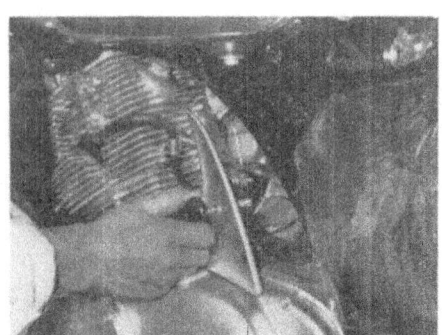

Fig. 5

5.

L. frame dust shield

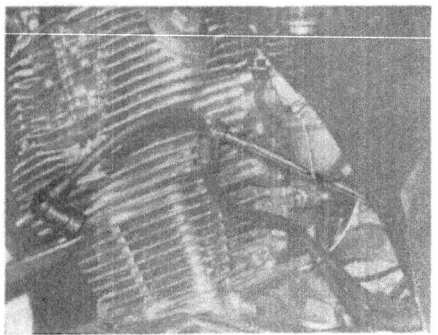

Fig. 6

6.

Plug cap

Air vent tube

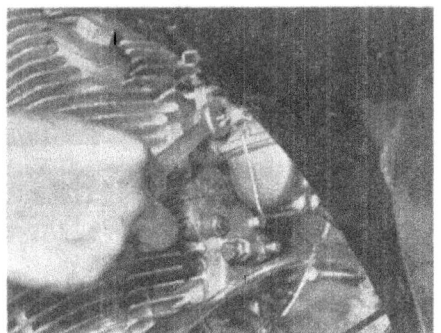

Fig. 7

7.

Carburetter setting nut   Fit securely

10 m/m spanner

Fig. 8

8.

Breather pipe   Tightening torque 2.1kgm (15ft. lb)   17 m/m socket wrench

Engine hanger bolt   Tightening torque 4.4kgm (32ft. lb)

17 m/m spanner

Disassembly	Assembly	Precaution	Tools
9. (R.-side) R. exhaust pipe joint nut	Tighten not to leak exhaust gas.	Refer to L. side	
10. R. exhaust pipe muffler		Refer to L. side	
11. R. step bar	Assemble with nutting in position at the puncn mark, tightening torque 2.1kgm (15ft. lb)	Refer to L. side	
12. Starting motor cable			10$^m/_m$ spanner

Fig. 9

	Disassembly	Assembly	Precaution Tools

13. R. dust shield

Refer to L. side
T-Handle forehead driver (#3)

Fig. 10

14. R. crank case cover

T-Handle forehead driver (#3)

10$^m/_m$ socket wrench

Fig. 11

15. Clutch wire

Fore driver

Fig. 12

16. Drive chain joint
Drive sprocket cover

Pliers

Disassembly	Assembly	Precaution Tools

17.

Chain joint clip

Fig. 13

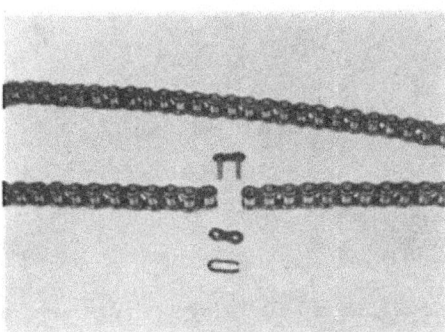

Fig. 14

18.

Engine wiring

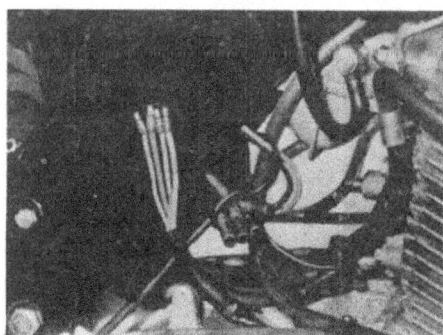

Fig. 15

19.

Plug cap

Air vent tube

Refer to L. side

Fig. 16

	Disassembly	Assembly	Precaution / Tools

Fig. 17

20. Carburetter setting nut

Set lever of fuel cup stop.

$10^m/_m$ spanner

Fig. 18

21. Engine hanger bolt

$17^m/_m$ socket wrench
$17^m/_m$ spanner

22. Engine setting bolt

$14^m/_m$ socket wrench

Fig. 19

23. The point of taking down engine

In case of fitting, be cautious not to damage on the front fender.

B. Cylinder

Disassembly	Assembly	Precaution	Tools

1. Condenser

$9^m/_m$ socket wrench

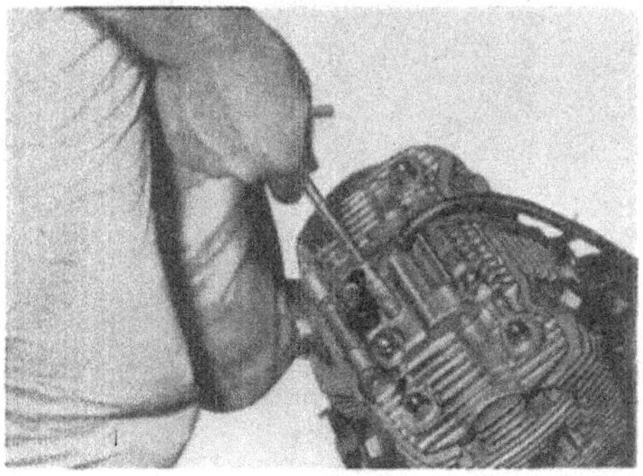

Fig. 20

2. Head cover

To tighten setting nuts on the head cover, follow order as shown here and repeat 2 to 3 times to tighten securely.
①②③④→white nut
⑤⑥⑦⑧→yellow nut

Pay attention to the color of nuts.

$14^m/_m$ socket wrench

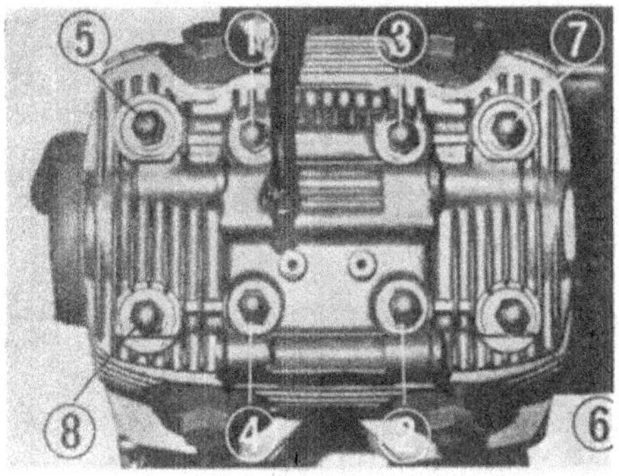

Fig. 21

3. Cam chain tensioner

$10^m/_m$ socket wrench

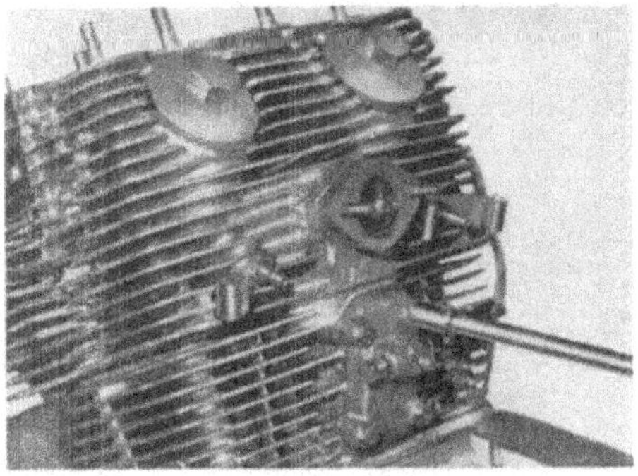

Fig. 22

4. Sparking plug

Plug socket wrench

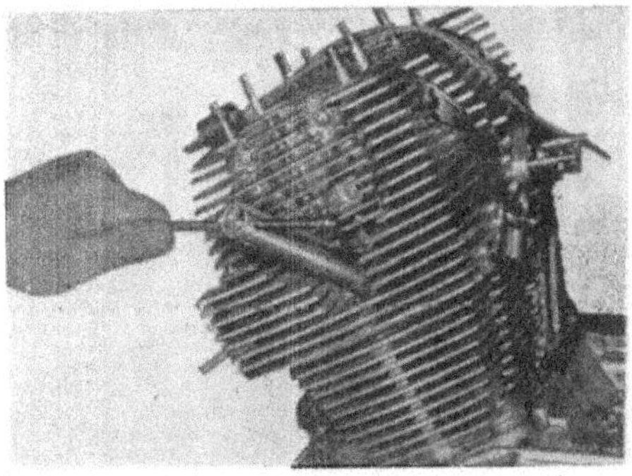

Fig. 23

	Disassembly	Assembly	Precaution Tools

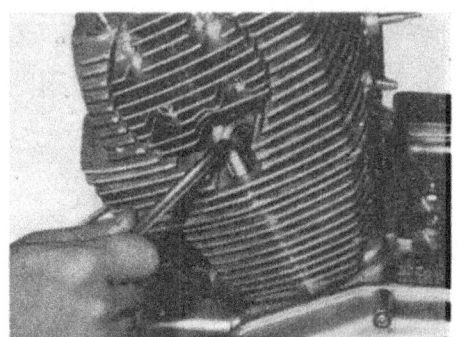

Fig. 24

6 m/m nut

steering top cone race box wrench

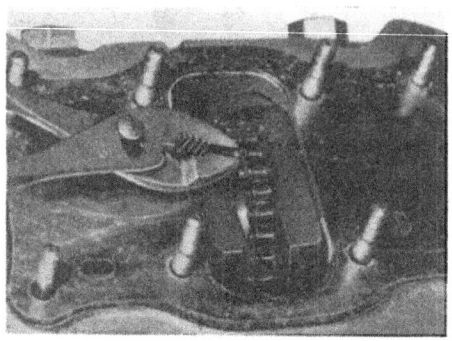

Fig. 25

5. Cam chain

Tightening torque 2.1kgm (15ft. lb)

In case of disassembly and fitting of the cam chain, be careful not to drop clip into the cylinder head.
Pliers

Fig. 26

Tie a wire at the end of chain to prevent chain from dropping into the cylinder.

Fig. 27

Fitting direction of clip; fit the joint to the direction of revolution of the crank (→)

Disassembly	Assembly	Precaution Tools

Combination process

① Coincide "T" punch mark on the dynamo rotor with the arrow mark on the starter.

14 m/m spanner

Fig. 28

② Coincide punch mark on the right tooth surface of the cam sprocket complete with the center line of the cylinder head, and combine sprocket of crank shaft by chain.

Fig. 29

6.
Cylinder head

Beforehand, valve rocker arm, cam shaft and valve should be subassembled.

Plastic hammer

Fig. 30

Pay attention to "O" ring and gasket.

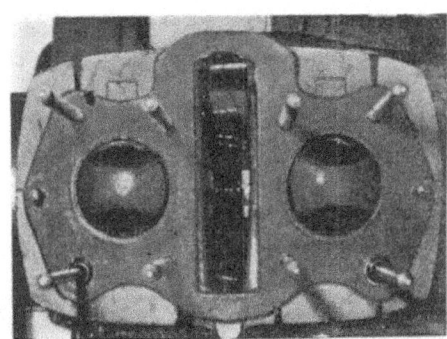

Fig. 31

	Disassembly	Assembly	Precaution Tools

Fig. 32

7.

Cylinder — In setting the cylinder on the piston, divide piston rings in 3 parts separately and put the ring retainer on the piston and push in the cylinder laying the stopper between piston and case. — Plastic hammer

Cylinder — Put in knock pin and packing securely.

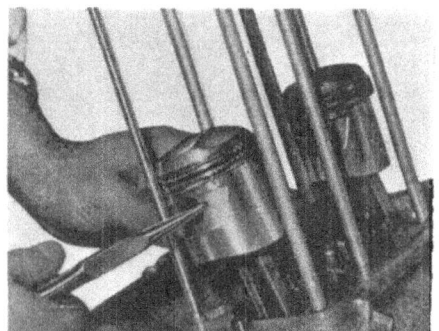

Fig. 33

8.

Piston — Use new piston pin clips, avoiding such clips lost elasticity. — Thin nose pliers

Fig. 34

In assemblying piston, put the punch mark on the head of piston to the foreward direction.

Disassembly	Assembly	Precaution Tools
	In fitting the piston, be careful on selection of clearance with cylinder previously. If the cylinder is over-sized, select piston fittable to this cylinder and assemble.	
9. Piston ring	After setting rings on the piston, check to avoid any hooking between ring and piston.	
	In fitting rings, be careful upper and lower surface of the rings. (Generally on the upper surface maker's punch mark is shown.)	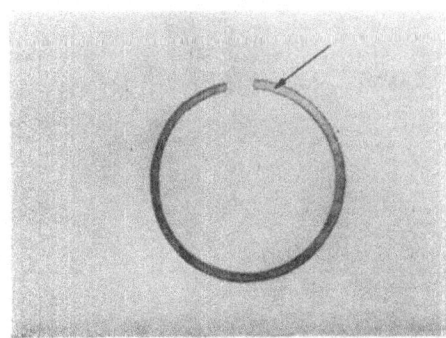 Fig. 35
	In case of using over sized cylinder, use a ring fittable with the cylinder.	

C. L. Cover

	Disassembly	Assembly	Precaution / Tools
 **Fig. 36**	1. L. cover Packing Dowel pin	In fitting L. cover, be careful the oil filter cover not to bite on a dowel pin of the oil filter shaft.	T-Handle forehead driver (#3) 10 m/m socket wrench Plastic hammer
 **Fig. 37**	2. Oil filter	Set oil filter drive sprocket pin facing R. outward.	
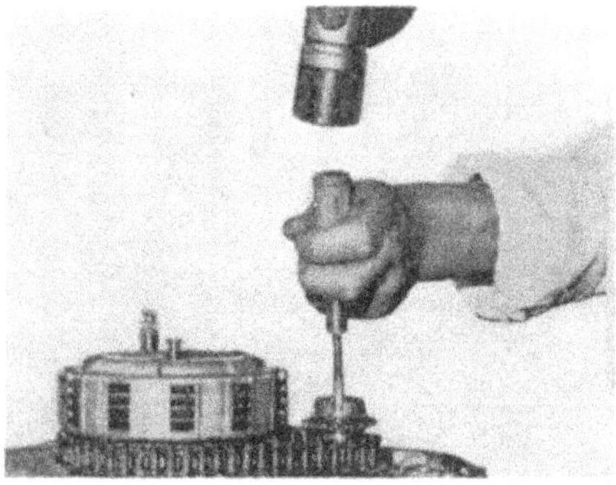 **Fig. 38**	3. Lock washer		Forehead driver Plastic hammer
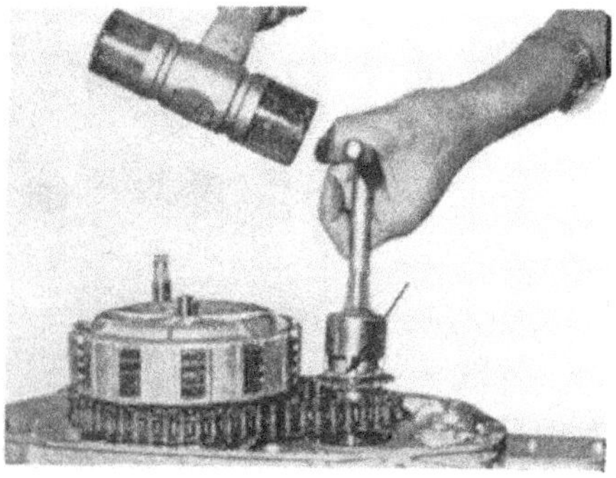 **Fig. 39**	4. Lock nut	After tightening perfectly, turn up the torque of lock washer. If not torque and nut coincided, nut should be locked after turning to the tightening direction without loosing it.	

Disassembly	Assembly	Precaution Tools

5.

Clutch pressure plate

To tighten plate setting bolts, tighten them evenly, diagonally as shown in the picture. Check existence of spring.

10 $^m/_m$ socket wrench

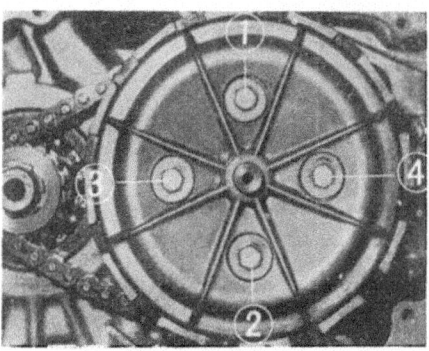

Fig. 40

6.

Clutch lifter joint piece

In assembly, check operation of oil metal guide.

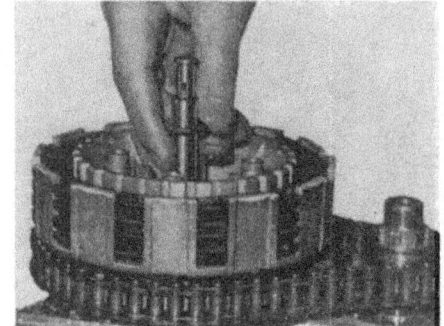

Fig. 41

7.

25 $^m/_m$ set ring

Be careful about cripple.

snap ring remover

Fig. 42

8.

Clutch center

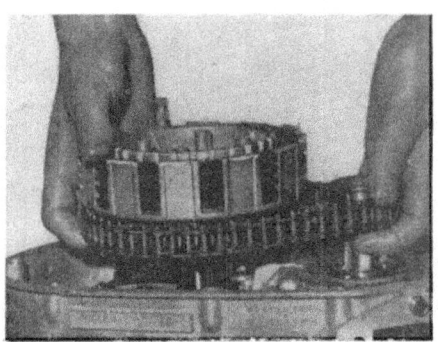

Fig. 43

	Disassembly	Assembly	Precaution Tools

Fig. 44

9.
Clutch plate
Clutch friction disc

Pay attention for order of fitting.

In disassembly and assembly, do it perpendicularly to the crank shaft and transmission main shaft.

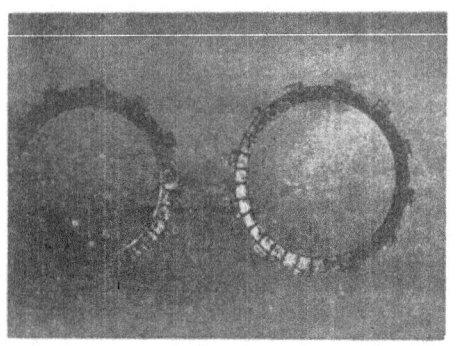

Fig. 45

Be careful about size.

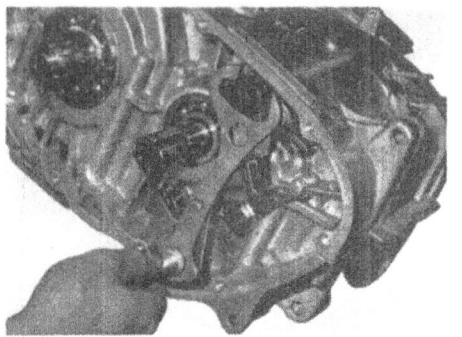

Fig. 46

10.
Shift spindle

Fig. 47

11.
Shift drum stopper
Shift drum stopper guide

10 $^m/_m$ socket wrench
17 $^m/_m$ socket wrench

Disassembly	Assembly	Precaution Tools

In tightening stopper bolt of kick starter, the mark on the end of kick starter spindle should be seen through the hole.

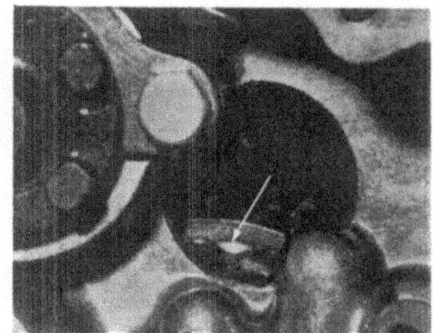

Fig. 48

D. R. Cover

	Disassembly	Assembly	Precaution Tools

Fig. 49

1.
Starting motor cable

10 m/m spanner

Fig. 50

2.
Starting motor
   R. L. side cover

T-Handle forehead driver (#2)

Fig. 51

3.
Starting motor

10 m/m socket wrench

Fig. 52

4.
Neutral switch

Disassembly	Assembly	Precaution Tools

5.

A.C. dynamo starter   After starter assembled, check rotation of the starter sprocket.

10 m/m socket wrench

Fig. 53

6.

A.C. dynamo Rotor

14 m/m socket wrench
Plastic hammer
Dynamo rotor puller
17 m/m spanner

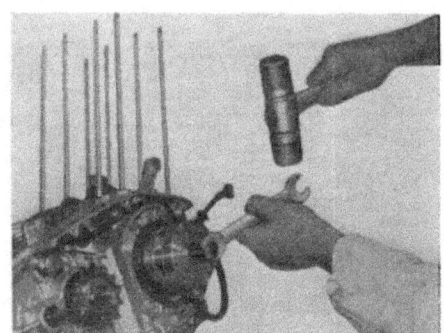

Fig. 54

7.

Starting sprocket stopper

10 m/m socket wrench
Plastic hammer
Forehead driver

Fig. 55

8.

Starter sprocket

Fig. 56

61

E. Mission (Crank)

	Disassembly	Assembly	Precaution Tools

Fig. 57

1. Upper crank case setting nut

14 m/m socket wrench

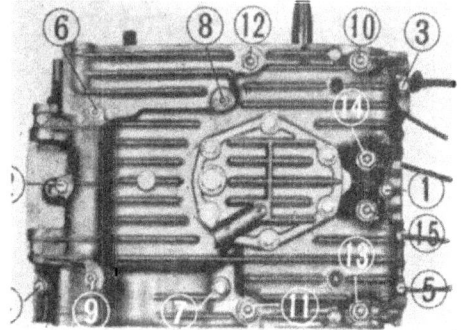

Fig. 58

2. Under crank case setting nut & bolt

In tightening nut and bolt. follow order as shown in figure starting temporary tightening and then actual tightening.

10 m/m socket wrench
14 m/m socket wrench
Plastic hammer

Fig. 59

3. Under crank case

Fig. 60

4. Main shaft

| Disassembly | Assembly | Precaution Tools |

5.

Counter shaft

Fig. 61

To set bearing oil seal, do it securely.

Fig. 62

Paint liquid packing on the case.

Note; lease the surface of packing before painting. Don't use with attaching cleansing oil or oil. Paint without choking oil holes.

Fig. 63

F. Cylinder Head

	Disassembly	Assembly	Precaution Tools

Fig. 64

1. Cylinder head cap

23 m/m spanner

Fig. 65

2. Contact breaker

T-Handle forehead driver (#2)

Fig. 66

3. R.L. cylinder head side cover

T-Handle forehead driver (#3)

Fig. 67

4. Tappet adjusting screw

10 m/m spanner
Tappet adjusting socket wrench

Disassembly	Assembly	Precaution / Tools

5.
Valve

Attach tag on L and R. valves not to be mixed each other.
Valve lifter
Thin nose pliers

Fig. 68

6.
Rocker arm crank pin
Rocker arm

In assembly rock arm crank pin, pay attention to outer diameter of inlet rocker arm crank pin and of exhaust rocker arm pin to insert inside the cylinder head. Former pin is larger than diameter of that of the latter.

Rocker arm crank pin extrator

Fig. 69

Cutting-grooves on the rocker arm crank pin at two places are set for oil passage and retreat for stud bolt. So need special attention to allocate pin to assemble.

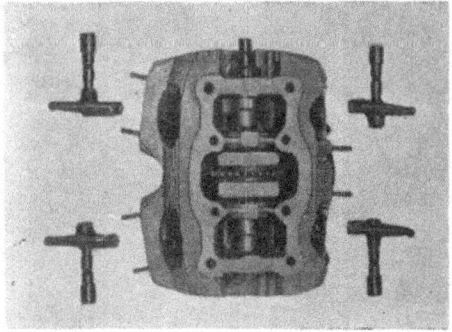

Fig. 70

7.
Cam shaft lock nut

Forehead driver
Plastic hammer

Fig. 71

| Disassembly | Assembly | Precaution Tools |

Fig. 72

8.

R. cam shaft

Forehead driver
Plastic hammer

Fig. 73

Assembly process of L. cam shaft. After coinciding spline, put the red line of the point shaft cam on the punched mark of the cam sprocket (facing upward) then insert.

Plastic hammer

Fig. 74

9.

Cam shaft lock nut
L. cam shaft

10 $^m/_m$ socket wrench

Fig. 75

10.

In assembly the cam shaft, coincide the spot where a tooth of spline of the cam sprocket complete is lacking with the corresponding spot on the cam shaft and then insert.

Disassembly	Assembly	Precaution Tools

11.

Cam sprocket comp. Put the punched mark upward and cam shaft rocker nut to the right side.

Fig. 76

Valve seat cutter

Fig. 77

G. Oil Pump

	Disassembly	Assembly	Precaution Tools

Fig. 78

Fig. 79

1.

Oil pump strainer
Oil pump packing B
Oil receiver
Oil pump body

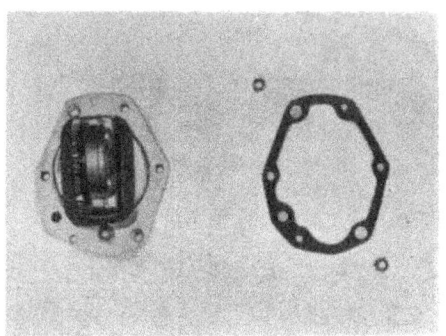

Fig. 80

2.

Oil pump packing A
Dowel pin

Fig. 81

3.

Snap ring

Check smooth running
of the drive gear.

Snap ring remover

Disassembly	Assembly	Precaution Tools
4. Side cover		Refer to the engine minor overhaul and assembly. T-Handle forehead driver (#3)
5. Oil pump side cover dowel pin Oil pump gear A Oil pump gear B Oil pump drive gear		

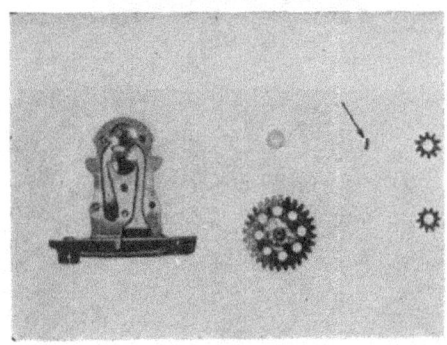

Fig. 82

2. ENGINE (CB72·77)

A. Engine replacement

	Disassembly	Assembly	Precaution Tools

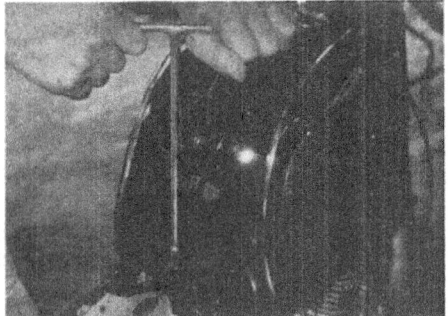

Fig. 83

1.
(L-side)
Dual seat

14 m/m spanner

Fig. 84

2.
Fuel tank setting bolt

10 m/m socket wrench

Fig. 85

Take out tubes A and B stopping choke.

Fig. 86

3.
Gear change pedal
Step bar

In assembly the step bar, coincide the punched mark with line of the bracket.

14 m/m socket wrench
10 m/m spanner

Disassembly	Assembly	Precaution Tools

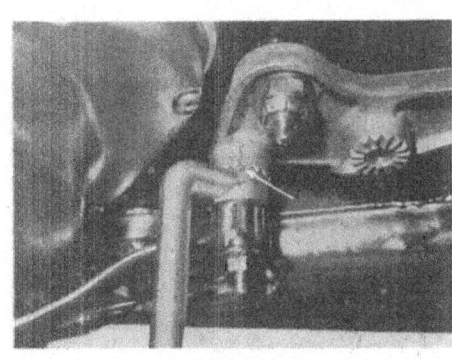
Fig. 87

4.
L. exhaust pipe joint nut
L. exhaust muffler

$10^{m/m}$ socket wrench
$14^{m/m}$ socket wrench
$14^{m/m}$ spanner (2)

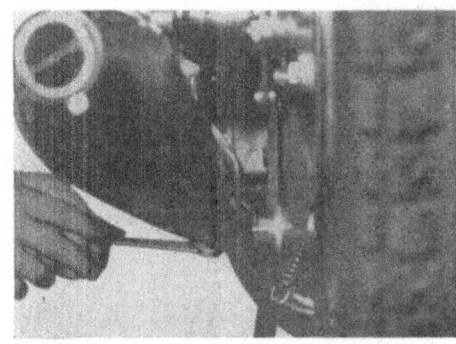
Fig. 88

5.
Upper crank case cover

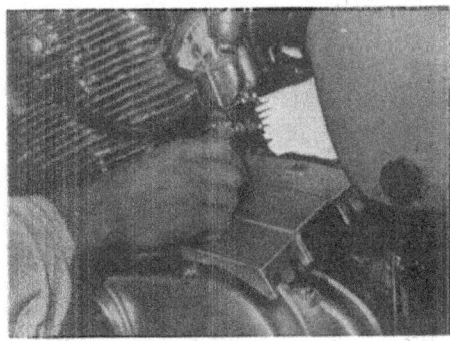
Fig. 89

6.
Speed-tachometer cable

$17^{m/m}$ spanner

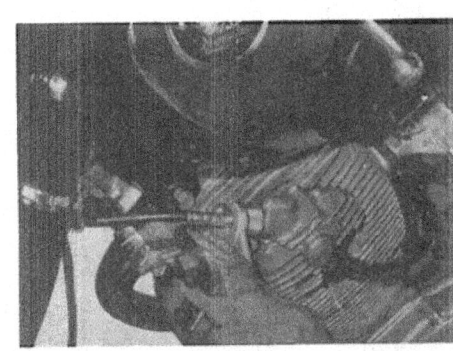
Fig. 90

	Disassembly	Assembly	Precaution Tools

Fig. 91

7.

L. air cleaner cover

Starting motor cable

10 m/m spanner

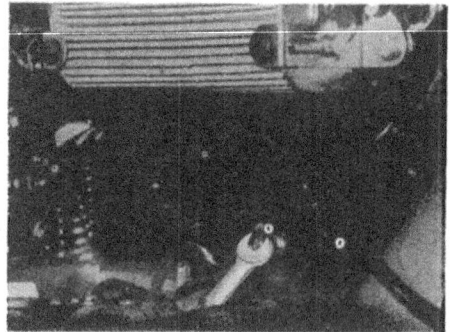

Fig. 92

8.

Air cleaner connecting tube

Throttle wire (refer to L. side)

T-Handle forehead driver (#2)

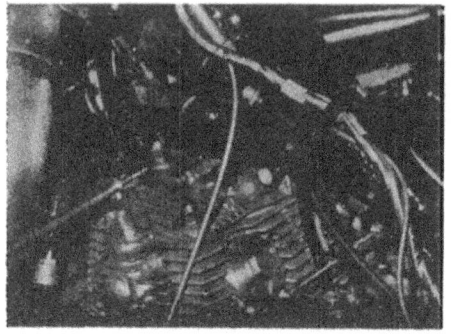

Fig. 93

9.

Engine setting bolt

17 m/m socket wrench

Fig. 94

10.

(R. side)

Brake pedal

Step bar

Stop switch

14 m/m socket wrench

Refer to L. side

Disassembly	Assembly	Precaution / Tools
11. R. exhaust pipe joint nut R. exhaust muffler		10 m/m socket wrench 14 m/m " 14 m/m spanner Refer to L. side
12. Dynamo cover		T-Handle forehead driver (#2)

Fig. 95

13. R. crank case cover Clutch wire Drive sprocket cover		T-Handle forehead driver (#3) Forehead driver

Fig. 96

14. Drive chain		Pliers Refer to the item of frame.

	Disassembly	Assembly	Precaution Tools

15.

Air cleaner case

Fig. 97

16.

Throttle wire

Fig. 98

17.

Aircleaner connecting tube

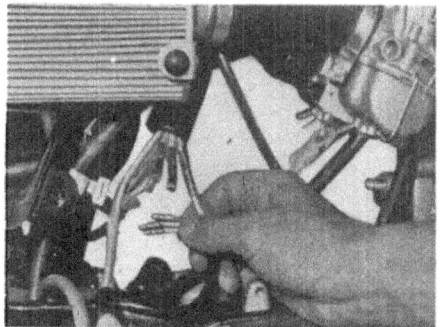

Fig. 99

18.

Engine wiring

About throttle wire refer to the item of Engine Replacement for Model CB 72, 77
T-Handle forehead driver (#2)

Disassembly	Assembly	Precaution / Tools
19. Contact breaker cover Contact breaker		T-Handle forehead driver (#2)

Fig. 100

20. Engine hanger bolt		17 m/m socket wrench 17 m/m spanner

Fig. 101

21. Engine setting bolt		Insert T-Handle forehead driver. Take out the former driver and lay down engine to take out the latter driver. 14 m/m spanner 14 m/m socket wrench 17 m/m spanner

B. Cylinder

	Disassembly	Assembly	Precaution Tools
	1. Carburetter		10 m/m spanner
	2. Cylinder head cover Cam chain tensioner		Refer to Model C72. 77 Engine Replacement.

Fig. 102

C. Engine minor overhaul and assembly

Disassembly	Assembly	Precaution Tools	
1. R. L. Cylinder head side cover		T-Handle forehead driver (#3)	 Fig. 103

3. FRAME (CB72 · 77)

A. Rear Fork

	Disassembly	Assembly	Precaution Tools
 Fig. 104	1. Rear brake wire comp.		14 m/m spanner
 Fig. 105	2. Rear brake stopper arm		Pliers. 14 m/m spanner
 Fig. 106	3. Cotter Pin Axle nut		Pliers
 Fig. 107	4. Rear wheel axle		Plastic namme.

| Disassembly | Assembly | Precaution | Tools |

5.

Drive chain

Fig. 108

6.

Rear wheel

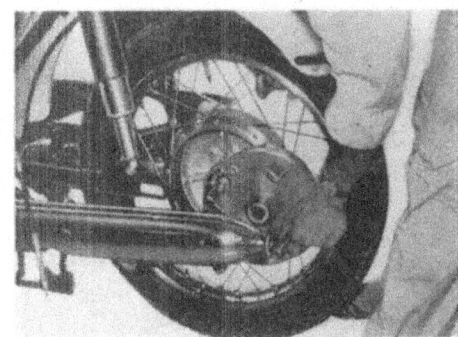

Fig. 109

7.

Chain case

10 m/m spanner
10 m/m socket wrench

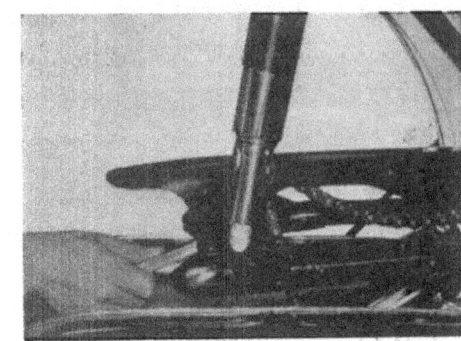

Fig. 110

8.

R. rear cushion

17 m/m socket wrench
17 m/m spanner

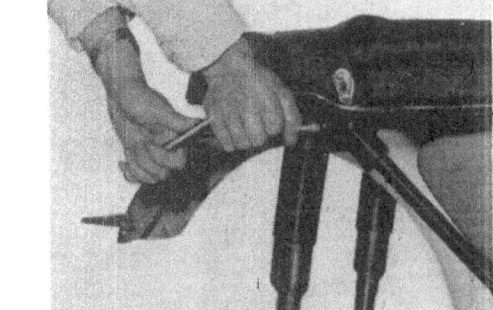

Fig. 111

	Disassembly	Assembly	Precaution Tools

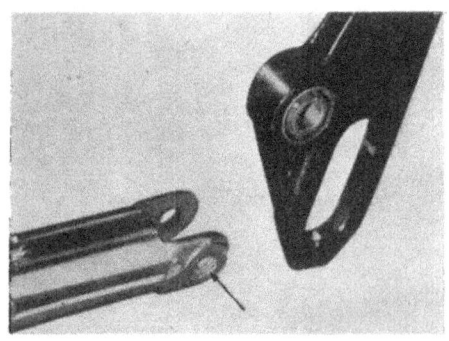

Fig. 112

In assembly, put the screwed side of the rear cushion under bolt hole to face outward.

9.
Exhaust muffler
Change pedal
Brake pedal
Step bar

Refer to the previously mentioned items of Engine Replacement.

Fig. 113

10.
R. step bar bracket

17 m/m socket wrench

Fig. 114

11.
L. step bar bracket

17 m/m socket wrench
Plastic hammer

B. Front fork

Disassembly	Assembly	Precaution / Tools	
1. Head light		T-Handle forehead driver (#2)	 Fig. 115
2. Wiring		Draw out only white, red and blue wires.	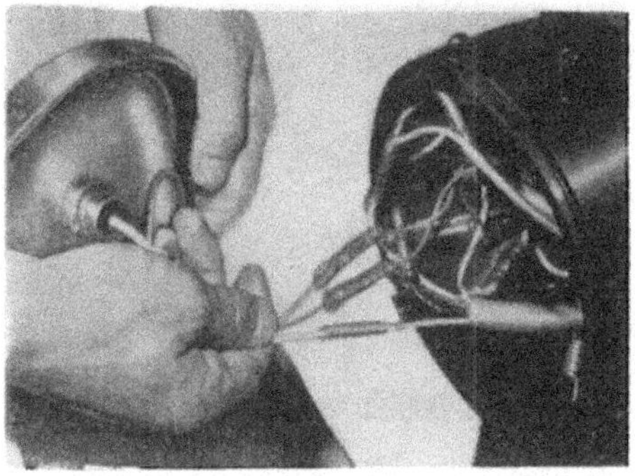 Fig. 116
3. Wire Harness terminal			 Fig. 117
4. Speedometer cable Tachometer cable		Pliers	 Fig. 118

	Disassembly	Assembly	Precaution Tools

Fig. 119

5.

Brake wire

14 m/m spanner

Fig. 120

6.

Front brake stopper arm

Plastic hammer
Forehead driver

Fig. 121

7.

Speedometer cable ass'y

Pliers

Fig. 122

Disassembly	Assembly	Precaution Tools	
8. Cotter pin (3×28) Front wheel axle nut		Pliers 23m/m socket wrench	 Fig. 123
9. Front wheel axle		14m/m spanner Plastic hammer	 Fig. 124
10. Front fork comp. Front fender		10m/m spanner	 Fig. 125
11. Starter switch ass'y		H-handle forehead driver (#2)	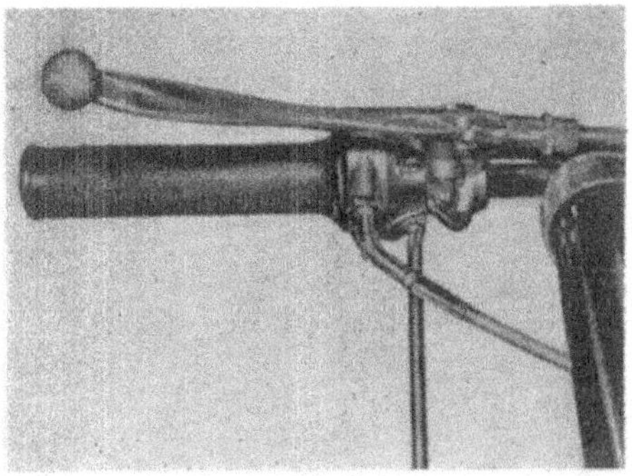 Fig. 126

	Disassembly	Assembly	Precaution Tools

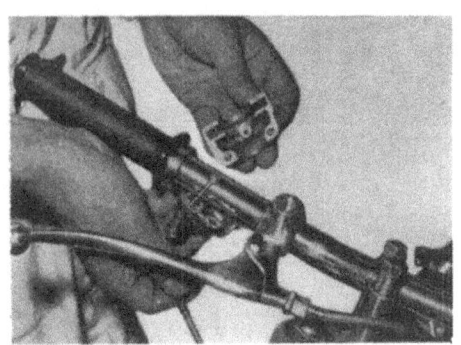

Fig. 127

12.

Throttle grip pipe

T-Handle forehead driver (#2)

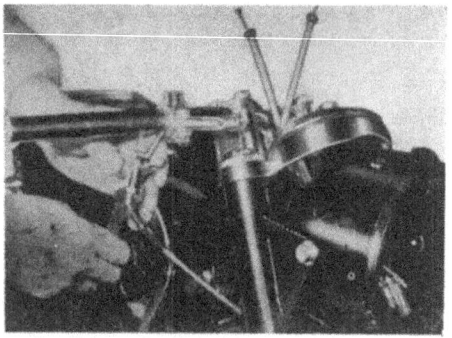

Fig. 128

13.

Throttle wire comp.

14 $^m/_m$ spanner

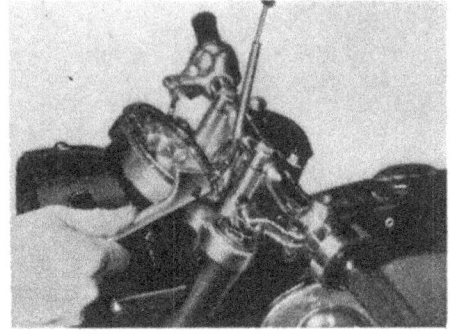

Fig. 129

14.

Clutch wire comp.
Front brake wire comp.
Clutch wire adjust bolt.
Fixing nut

Pliers

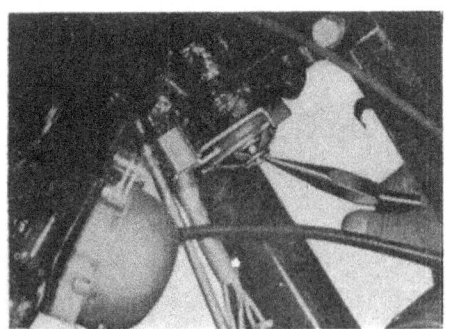

Fig. 130

15.

Snap pin 6 $^m/_m$
Steering damper
{ lock spring nut
  spring
  Plate
  Friction disk

Pliers

84

Disassembly	Assembly	Precaution Tools

16.
Hex. bolt 8×30
Steering handle pipe comp.

In assembly, pay attention on punched mark.

14 m/m socket wrench

Fig. 131

17.
Steering damper
{ knob comp.
{ lock spring
Damper lock spring set bolt.

17 m/m socket wrench

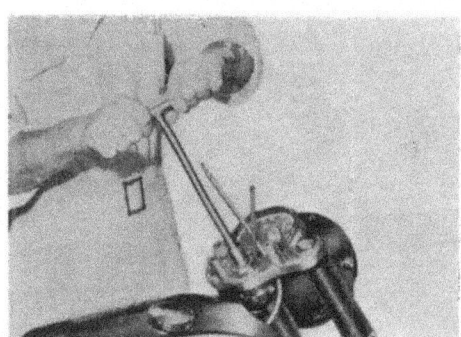
Fig. 132

18.
Speedometer ass'y

Fig. 133

19.
Front fork bolt
Steering head stem nut.
Stem nut

26 m/m spanner
35 m/m spanner

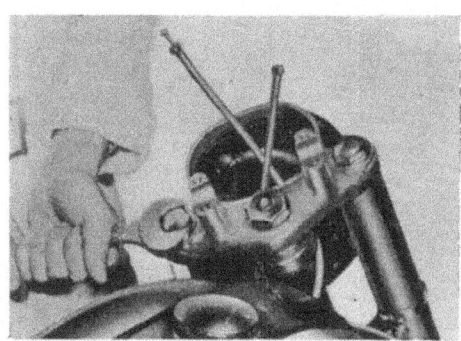
Fig. 134

	Disassembly	Assembly	Precaution Tools

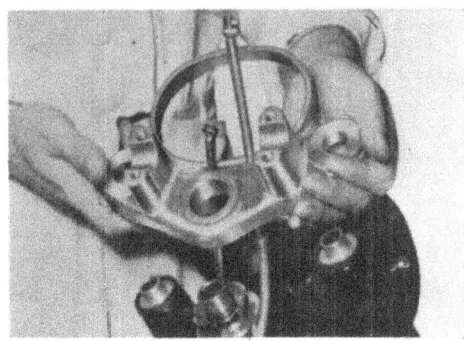

Fig. 135

20.

Fork top bridge

Fig. 136

21.

Steering head thread comp.

Steering top corn race

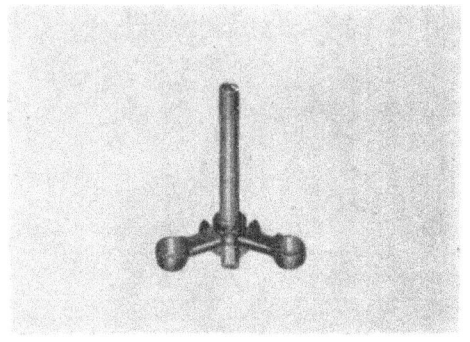

Fig. 137

22.

Steering stem comp.

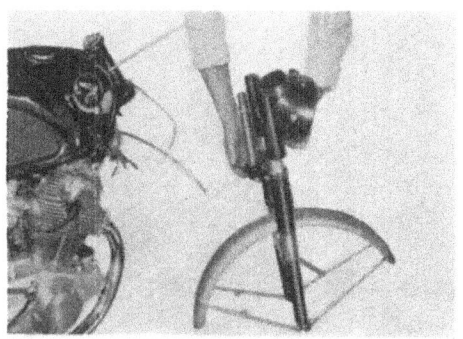

Fig. 138

Disassembly	Assembly	Precaution Tools

23.
Front fender

Take out an arrow marked bolt.

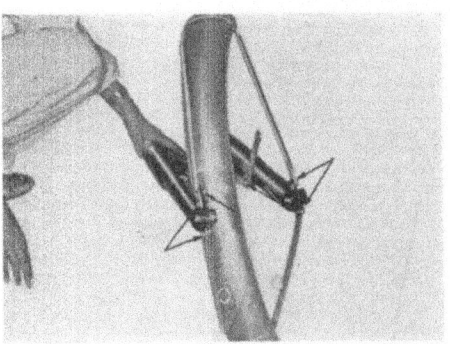
Fig. 139

24.
Front fork comp.

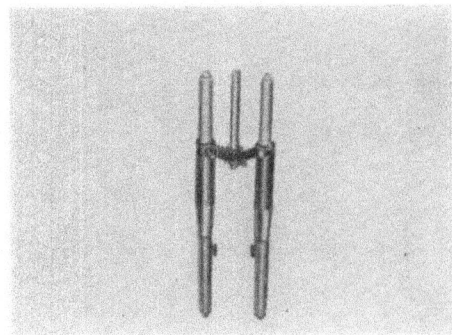
Fig. 140

Put the front fork under cover with welded clip as the R side

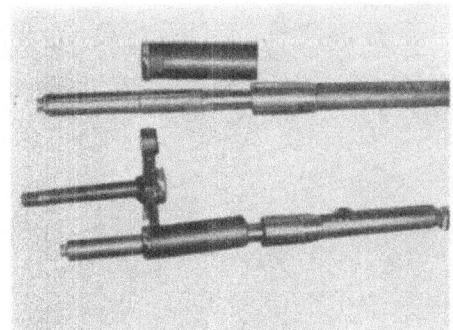
Fig. 141

CONSTRUCTION

CONTENTS

1. DIFFERENCE BETWEEN C72·77 & CB72·77
    - A. Engine 93
    - B. Frame 93
2. ENGINE
    - A. Main Parts of Engine 95
    - B. Lubricating System 97
    - C. Centrifugal Oil Filter 99
3. POWER TRANSMISSION
    - A. Clutch and Primary Chain 100
    - B. Transmission System 103
    - C. Final Drive Mechanism 109
4. AUXILIARY PARTS
    - A. Funnel Type Breather 110
    - B. Kick Starter Mechanism 110
    - C. Cam Chain Tensioner 111
5. CARBURETTOR 113
6. FRAME 118
7. SUSPENSION
    - A. Front Wheel Suspension 120
    - B. Rear Wheel Suspension 121
8. STEERING SYSTEM
    - A. Handle 123
    - B. Steering 124
9. BRAKE INSTALLATION
10. WHEEL
    - A. Front Wheel 128
    - B. Rear Wheel 129
11. AUXILIARY EQUIPMENT
    - A. Air Cleaner 131
    - B. Muffler 132

CONSTRUCTION

1. POINTS OF CONSTRUCTIONAL DIFFERENCE BETWEEN HONDA 250, 300 MODEL C72, 77 AND CB72, 77.

Honda 250, 300 super sport Model CB72, 77 has a newly designed chassis equipped with engine which partly reconstructed from that of Model C72, 77, and aimed mainly to be used as sports car maintaining availability as racer interchanging some of its parts. As this engine is high rotation, high power type and chassis is light weight, high rigidity type, the special constructional featurer comparing with Model C72, 77 could be cited as follow.

A. Engine

1. Twin carburetor

   To raise horse power adopted Twin carburetor system removing junction of suction manifold.

2. Reciprocating change

   Change control system suitable for high speed running and racing.

3. Kick of forward **step**

   Considering relation with frame, direction of step of kick arm was set forward.

4. 180 degree (I-Type) crank angle

   To get stability at high speed reducing vibration left and right crank arm angle was set as 180 degrees.

B. Frame

1. Frame and rear fork of steel tubing

   To attain light weight and raise rigidity main constructional member is constructed by high carbon steel pipes.

2. Telescopic type fork

   To raise stability at high speed running on rough road maintaining rigidity, Telescopic type fork was adopted on the front wheel suspension.

3. Rear cushion of three step adjustment

   Rear cushion is adjustable according to load and road condition.

4. 18 inch type

   To enlarge bank angle and to help pleasant feeling on rough road, equipped with front wheel 2.75–18, and rear wheel 3.00–18.

5. **Speed Tachometer**

   Speedmeter and Tachometer were set in the same case.

6. **Step and handle easy to move or interchange**

   To make easy riding posture suitable for general, high speed or race riding.

MEMO

2. ENGINE

A. Main parts of engine

Cylinder and Cylinder Head are the most important parts of engine and its construction, material and its machining rate of precision affect engine performance.

This type of engine adopted most suitable O.H.V. type valve arrangement to attain efficient combustion chamber form. On the other hand the camshaft is set in the cylinder head and the valves are actuated by Locker arm (O.H.C.), accordingly reciprocating parts are reduced very much comparing with other types.

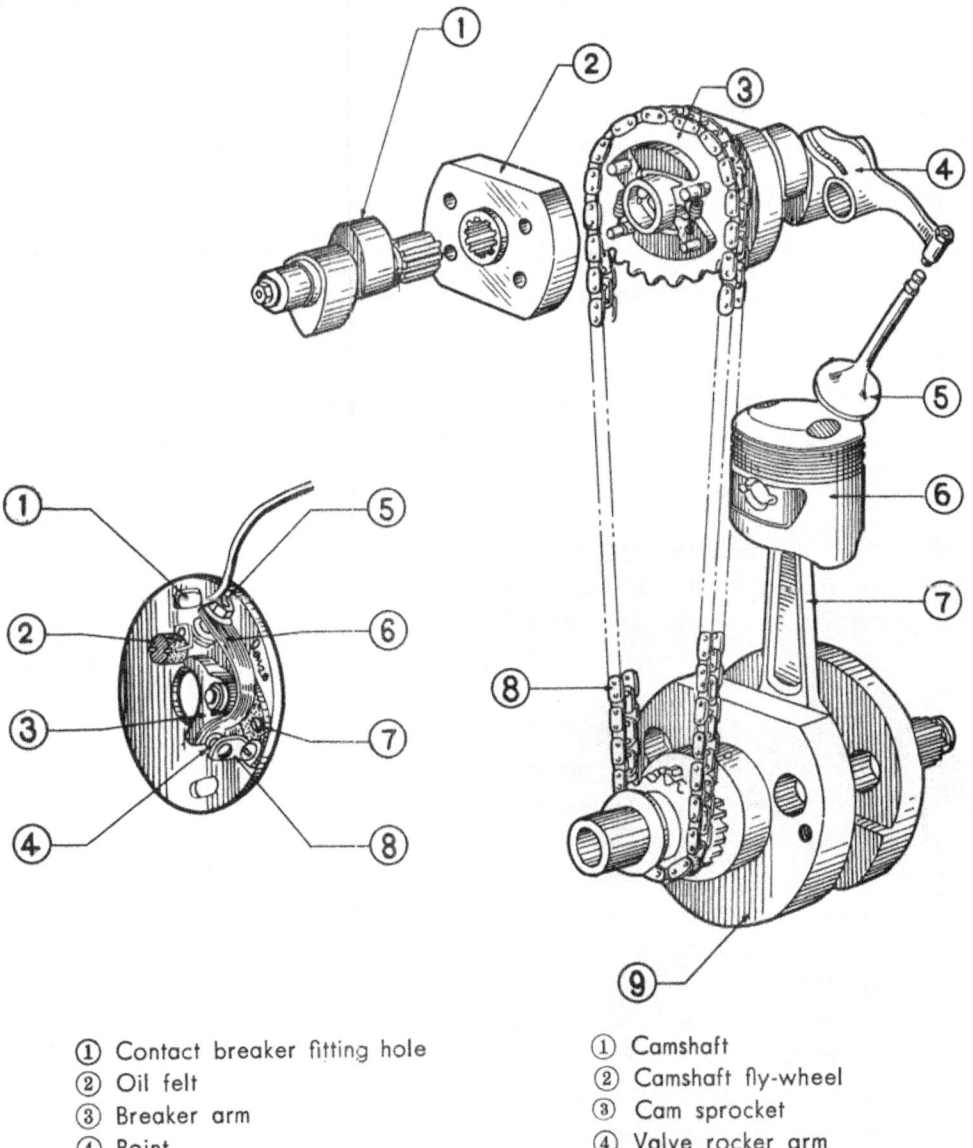

① Contact breaker fitting hole
② Oil felt
③ Breaker arm
④ Point
⑤ Terminal
⑥ Spring
⑦ Screw to fix contact point
⑧ Contact point

① Camshaft
② Camshaft fly-wheel
③ Cam sprocket
④ Valve rocker arm
⑤ Valve
⑥ Piston
⑦ Connecting rod
⑧ Cam chain
⑨ Crankshaft

Fig. 2-1.

The cam shaft is driven by chain through the timing gear reductioned 1/2. As the cylinder head is made of light alloy, not only it is light but cooling efficiency is excellent as heat conductivity is good, and shape of combustion chamber is ideal semi-spherical one to get efficient combustion of mixture and also to attain larger compression ratio.

As the cylinder is machined with high rate of precision cooling efficiency and lubrication are favorable, accordingly wearing effect is very small. Single row W type Needle Bearing is used at the big end of the connecting rod to get ample loading capacity at the bearing.

On the other hand single row Ball Bearings are used on the crankshaft, where W type middle parts at 2 stations single row the needle bearing are used to get larger loading capacity.

As crankshaft has an important function to convert reciprocating motion to rotation, inertia force due to reciprocating motion of piston and connecting rod should be reduced by putting balance weight to get smooth revolution. The crankshaft can rotate smooth running as it is balanced by dynamic balance on the balancing machine after complete maching.

To reduce vibration at high speed revolution and to get stability at high speed running the right and left crank arm angle of Model CB72, CB77-I crankshaft is set 180 degree. (For Model C72, C77-II type angle is 360 degree)

Fig. 2-2. Type-I crankshaft

① Piston
② Roller bearing
③ Connecting rod
④ R-crankshaft
⑤ 6205 Z special ball bearing
⑥ Cam chaim sprocket
⑦ L. crank shaft
⑧ Oil pump drive gear

Fig. 2-3. Type-II crankshaft

B. Lubricating system

Construction and Operation

For Honda 250, 300 oil is supplied under pressure by gear pump and wet-sump system is applied. The oil pump is attached under crankcase by 6 bolts. The oil pump is shown in Fig. 2-5 and (1) is driving gear and (2) driven gear. Power is transmitted by driving gear (3) meshing with crankshaft gear. As for operation of gear pump, the driving gear (1) rotates to the arrow direction and the driven gear (2) rotates counterwise, then degree of vacuum increases on the right side sucking oil from this side to feed the left side.

Therefore each part of the pump should be carefully inspected to avoid engine burning or other troubles due to mal lubrication. Such troubles after occur due to oil leakage through inadequate gap between gear teeth and pump main body, or between gear face and pump body or pump side cover causing drop of degree of vacuum.

Lubricating oil sumped in the crankcase is sucked by oil pump to pass through the

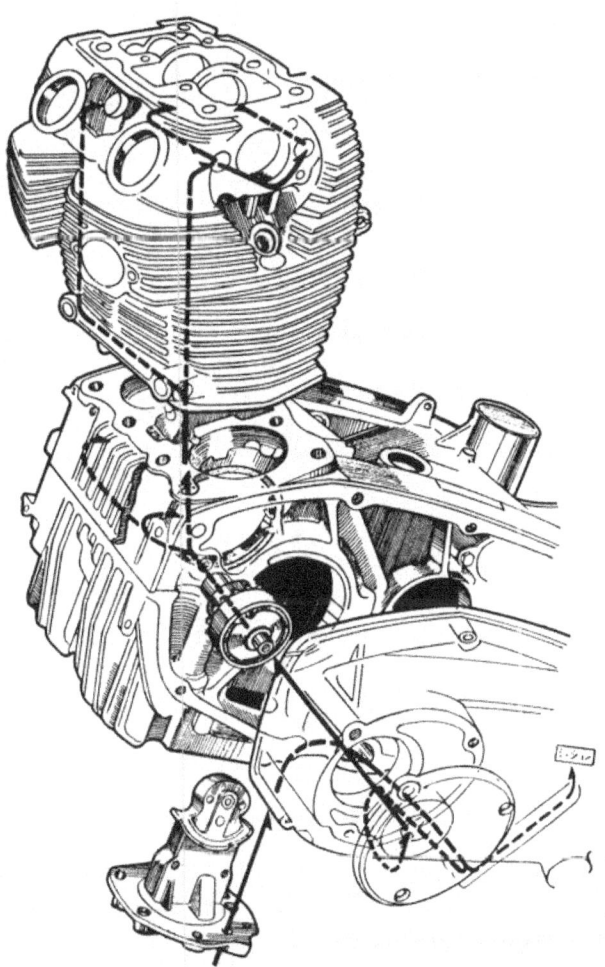

Fig. 2-4. Lubricating Circulation

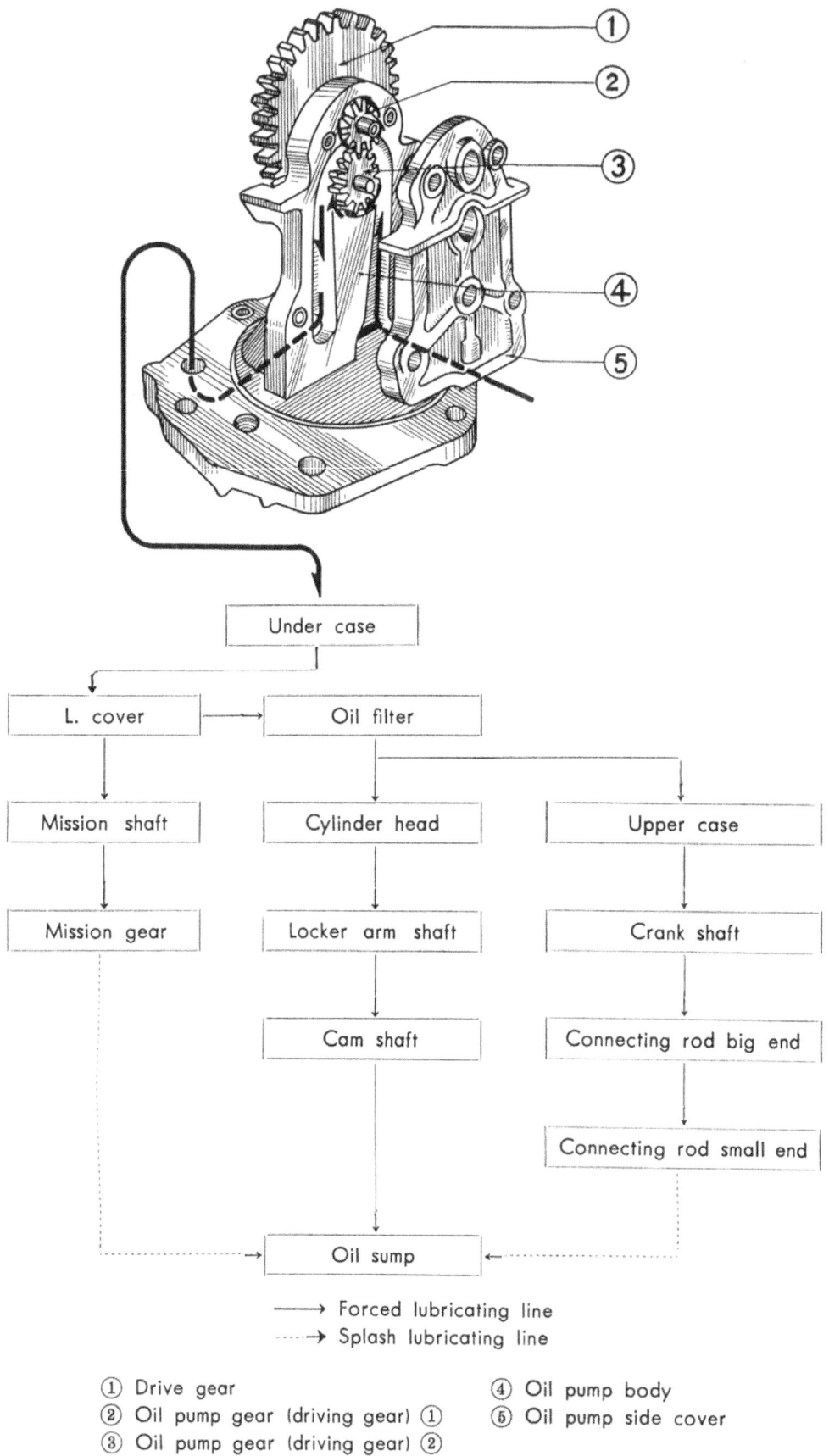

```
                    Under case
                        │
         ┌──────────────┼──────────────┐
         ▼              ▼              
    L. cover  ───▶  Oil filter
         │              │              │
         ▼              ▼              ▼
   Mission shaft   Cylinder head    Upper case
         │              │              │
         ▼              ▼              ▼
   Mission gear   Locker arm shaft  Crank shaft
                        │              │
                        ▼              ▼
                    Cam shaft    Connecting rod big end
                                       │
                                       ▼
                                Connecting rod small end

                      Oil sump
```

⟶ Forced lubricating line
┈⟶ Splash lubricating line

① Drive gear
② Oil pump gear (driving gear) ①
③ Oil pump gear (driving gear) ②
④ Oil pump body
⑤ Oil pump side cover

Fig. 2-5.

under crankcase and L-crankcase cover then the pipe line in splitted to 2-ways, one to the oil filter.

Oil cleaned in the oil filter is feeded to the crankcase where the line is splitted again to 2-ways, one is guided to the crankshaft through the center bearing and lubricate the big end of connecting rod and also the small end by splashing, and another line is guided up to the cylinderhead along the cylinder stud bolts from the upper crank case to lubricate camshaft and locker arm separately in the front and rear rocker arm in in the head then drop in the crank case through the space around the cam chain.

On the other hand, one line splitted in the L-crank case cover is guided into the transmission mainshaft through the oil guide metal which is fixed on the L-crank case cover by spring, and then drop in the crank case lubricating mission gear through oil hole bored in the shaft.

C. Centrifugal oil filter

Oil Filter is located on the front side of L-crank case cover and oil is cleaned and separated by centrifugal force driven by the drive sprocket of the crank shaft and chain.

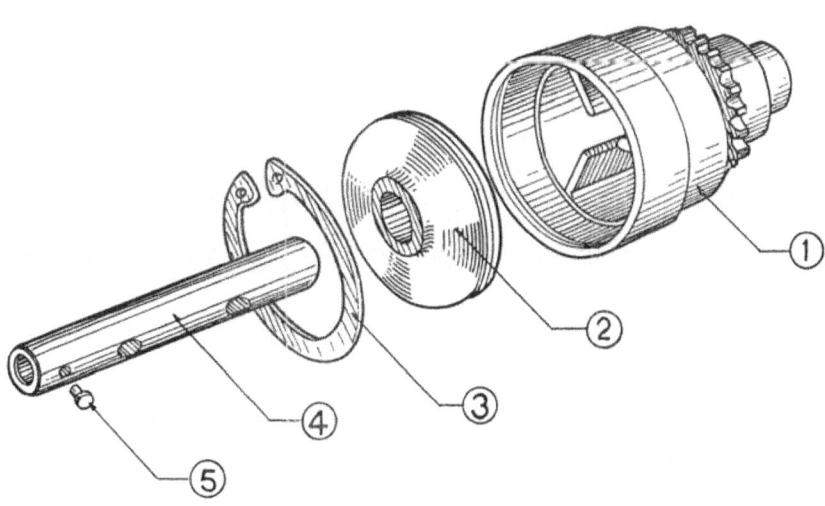

① Oil filter rotor 　④ Oil filter shaft
② Rotor cap 　　　⑤ Filter shaft stopper pin
③ 52mm circlip

Fig. 2-5.

3. POWER TRANSMISSION

Power transmission is defined such mechanism as rotation of crankshaft is transmitted to rear wheel. The first step of transmission from crankshaft to clutch is done by chain. This clutch is wet multiple plate type, so there is no heat generated by friction and also no noise perfectly.

As this transmission is such type of advance 4-step and constant meshing, there is no gear sound while in gear changing, and consequently made it possible to widen rear wheel driving power of powerful engine.

Further power is transmitted to the rear wheel sprocket by chain drive from the mission, and through rear wheel bumper of rubber made to the rear wheel sprocket and the rear wheel torque is transmitted between the final driven flange.

So that torque is transmitted very smoothly without chain knock getting smooth running. Especially as clutch is located on the mission shaft, made it possible to minimize de-deflection of crankshaft and also to stabilize clutch function reducing clutch inertia.

A. Clutch and primary chain

Clutch

(1) Function and kinds

Function of clutch is to cut or engage power transmission in case of changing gear or starting locating between the engine and the transmission mechanism. Therefore fineness of cutting and smoothness of engaging and disengaging are important feature.

There are several kinds of clutch system as cone clutch, centrifugal clutch, multi-plate clutch and single clutch, and we call wet type when merged in oil and dry system when oil is not used inside.

(2) Construction and function

For Honda 250, 300 we adopted type of wet multiplate clutch.

As shown in Fig. 3-1 (Disassembled figure) and Fig. 3-2 (cross sectional figure), there is clutch outer complete when crank case cover is taken out. In the clutch outer complete, clutch spring (10) in set by 4 of 6×24 hex bolts pressing clutch pressure plate (9) and sandwitching clutch friction disk (6) by clutch plate (7). Inside of the clutch plate teeth are cut which mesh with that of outer part of clutch center (8), and the clutch center is connected with the transmission mainshaft by spline and rotates with (8) (7) and (9) as a whole with the transmission mainshaft.

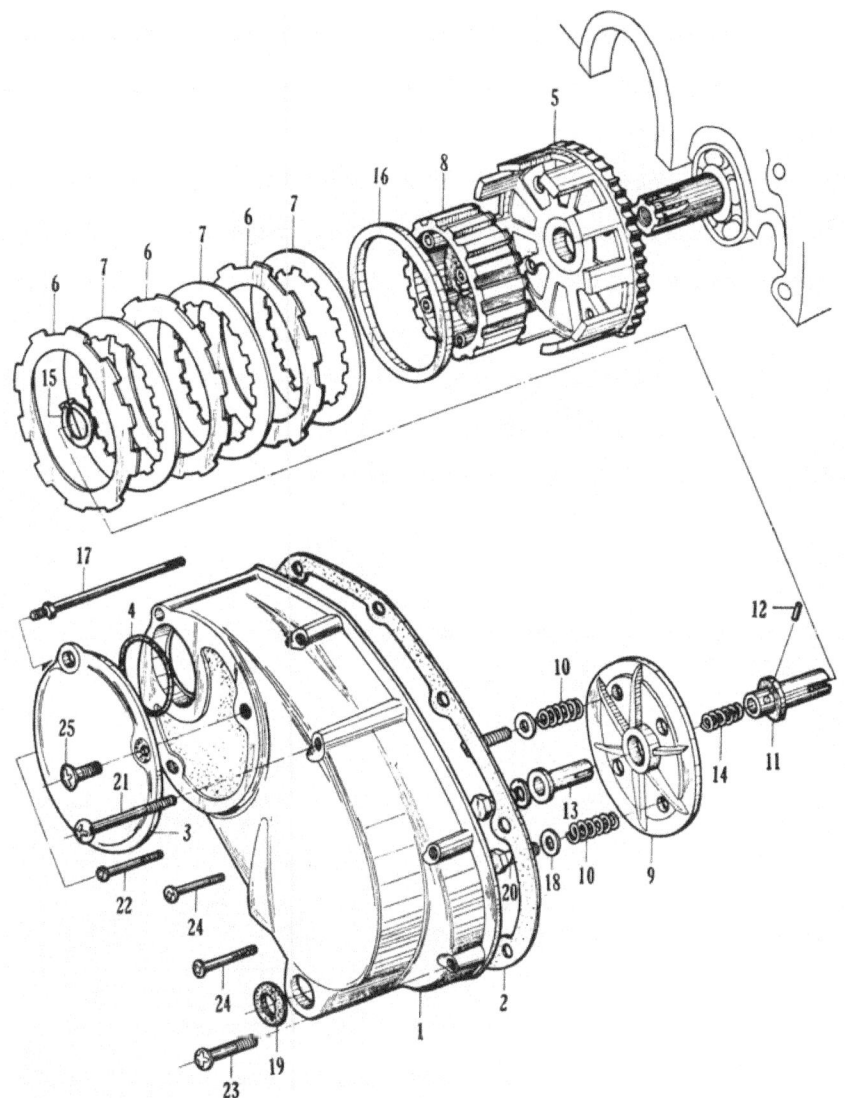

① L-crank case cover
② L-crank case cover packing
③ Oil filter cover
④ 57×3 O-ring
⑤ Clutch outer comp.
⑥ Clutch friction disk
⑦ Clutch plate
⑧ Clutch center
⑨ Clutch pressure plate
⑩ Clutch spring
⑪ Clutch lifter joint piece
⑫ Oil guide metal pin
⑬ Oil guide metal
⑭ Oil guide metal spring
⑮ 25 m/m circlip
⑯ L-leg sealed under bolt
⑰ 6×19 washer
⑱ 14257 oil seal
⑲ 6×24 Hex bolt
⑳ 6×74 cross head screw
㉑ 6×10   ″
㉒ 6×45   ″
㉓ 6×35   ″
㉔ 6×16   ″

Fig. 3-1. Disassembled picture of clutch

On the other hand, with the groove cut along the outer perimeter of clutch outer, the clutch friction disc is connected through flange mating with said groove, and the transmission main shaft can rotate freely.

Therefore in case of disengaging clutch, (9) (6) (7) (6) (7) (6) (7) (6) (7) (8) and (5) are pressed by clutch springs, rotating power of crank is transmitted to the mission as a whole by friction.

Inside of the clutch outer, the primary driven sprocket is fixed by rivetting and as primary chain is set on this sprocket, power is transmitted to the transmission main shaft through the primary chain from the crank.

Handle the clutch lever, the clutch lifter thread turns right by clutchwire, and the lifter thread is pushed out inside by the screw inside of clutch adjuster fixed on the R crank case and push outside the clutch lifter piece (11) through clutch lifter rod.

As the clutch pressure plate (9) is pushed onside by the clutch lifter joint piece, clutch spring (10) is compressed to free (6) (7) of each 4 pieces. Therefore rotation of (5) (6) (6) (6) (6) is not transmitted to (8).

[**Note**]

Number of clutch plate and clutch friction disk is four sheet each for Model C72 and 5 sheets each for Model C77, CB72, 77.

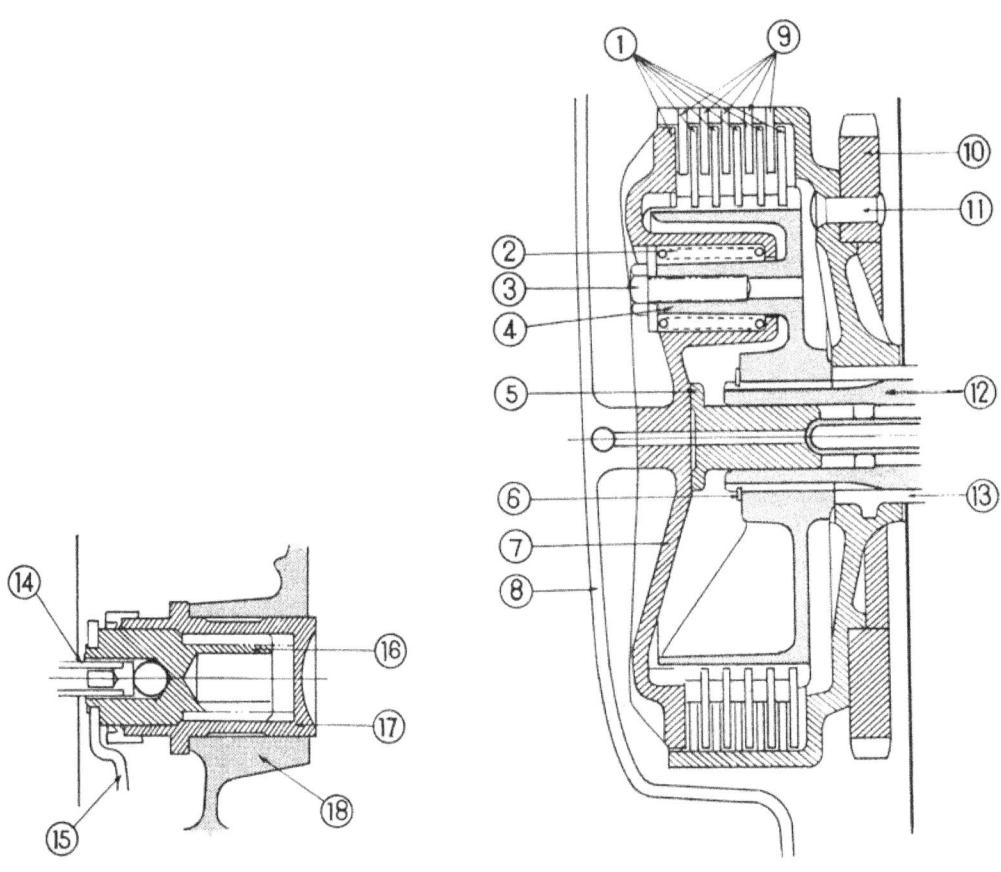

① Clutch plate
② Clutch spring
③ 6mm bolt
④ Clutch center
⑤ Clutch lifter joint piece
⑥ 25mm circlip
⑦ Pressure plate
⑧ L-crank case cover
⑨ Clutch friction disk
⑩ Primary driven sprocket
⑪ 6mm rivet
⑫ Mission shaft
⑬ Clutch outer boss
⑭ Clutch lifter rod
⑮ Clutch lever
⑯ Clutch lifter thread
⑰ Clutch adjuster
⑱ R-crank case cover

Fig. 3-2. Cross section of clutch for Model C72

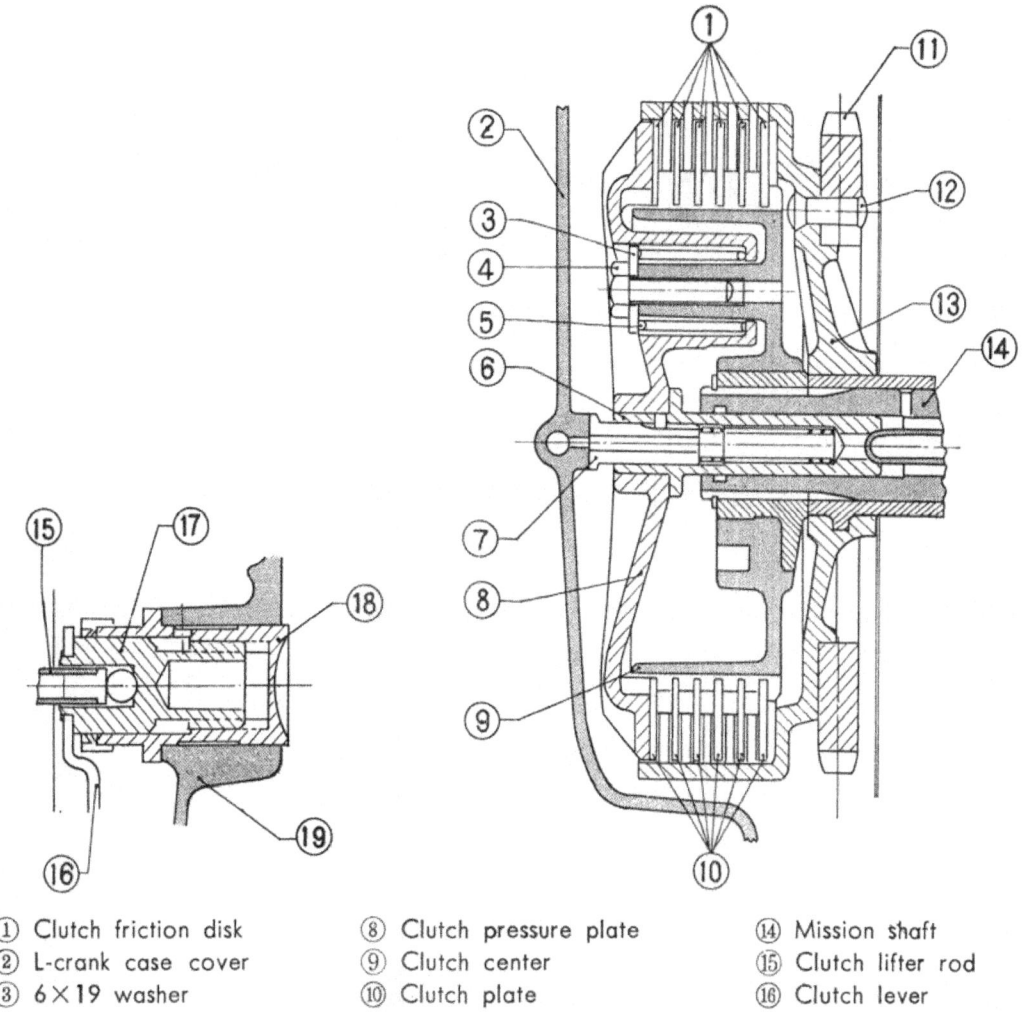

① Clutch friction disk
② L-crank case cover
③ 6×19 washer
④ 6×24 Hex.bolt
⑤ Clutch spring
⑥ Clutch lifter joint piece
⑦ Oil guide metal
⑧ Clutch pressure plate
⑨ Clutch center
⑩ Clutch plate
⑪ Printing driven sprocket
⑫ 6mm rivet
⑬ Clutch outer
⑭ Mission shaft
⑮ Clutch lifter rod
⑯ Clutch lever
⑰ Clutch lifter thread
⑱ Clutch adjuster
⑲ R crank case cover

Fig. 3-3. Cross section of clutch for Model C77, CB72, 77

B. Transmission system

1. Function and kinds.

Following clutch, function of transmission is to convey power transmission, and convert torque by means of meshing gears of different number of teeth. As shown in Fig. 3-4 if driving gear is smaller than driven gear, no. of rotation of the driven side will be smaller transmitting large torque. Here it is called reduction ratio showing the ratio of each gear numbers.

There are two systems of gear meshing for transmission of auto-bicycle i.e. · selective sliding system and constant meshing.

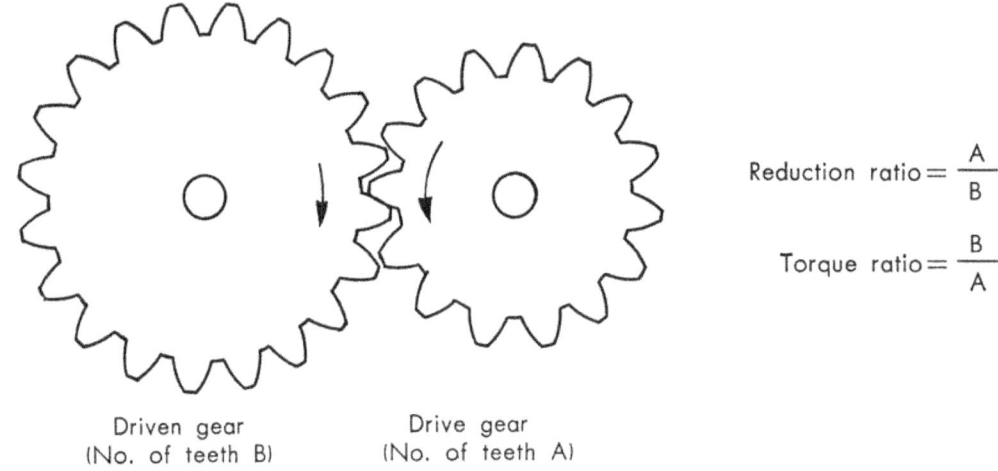

$$\text{Reduction ratio} = \frac{A}{B}$$

$$\text{Torque ratio} = \frac{B}{A}$$

Driven gear (No. of teeth B)   Drive gear (No. of teeth A)

Fig. 3-4. Relation between reduction ratio and torque ratio

By selective sliding system, shift gear is slided by gear shift fork to get adequate reduction ratio by changing gear to be meshed, and by constant meshing system, each gear can be rotated freely always each gear in meshing state, and can be changed reduction ratio by actuating optional gear by means of special clutch.

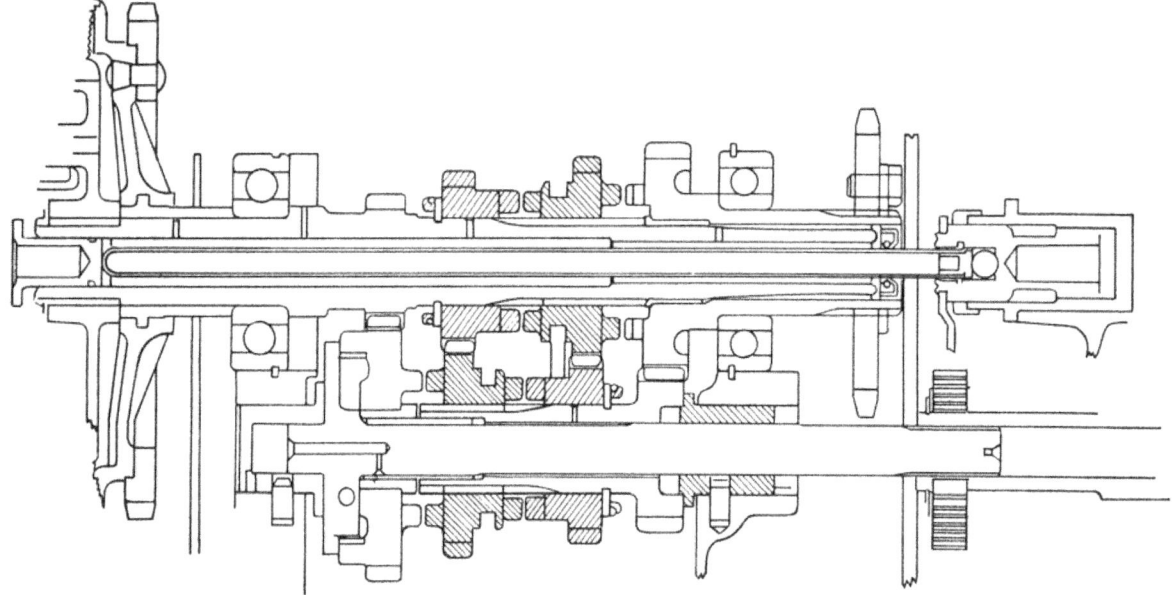

Fig. 3-5. Cross sectional figure of transmission gear

2. Construction and Function

The transmission system of Honda 250·300 is constant mesh and advance 4 stage rotary type. In Fig. 3-5 to Fig. 3-9, neutral, first, second, third and top stage are shown. Function of transmission as shown in Fig. 3-5 and Fig. 3-10 is as follows, i.e. power is transmitted from crank shaft to primary drive chain, clutch outer, clutch center and transmission.

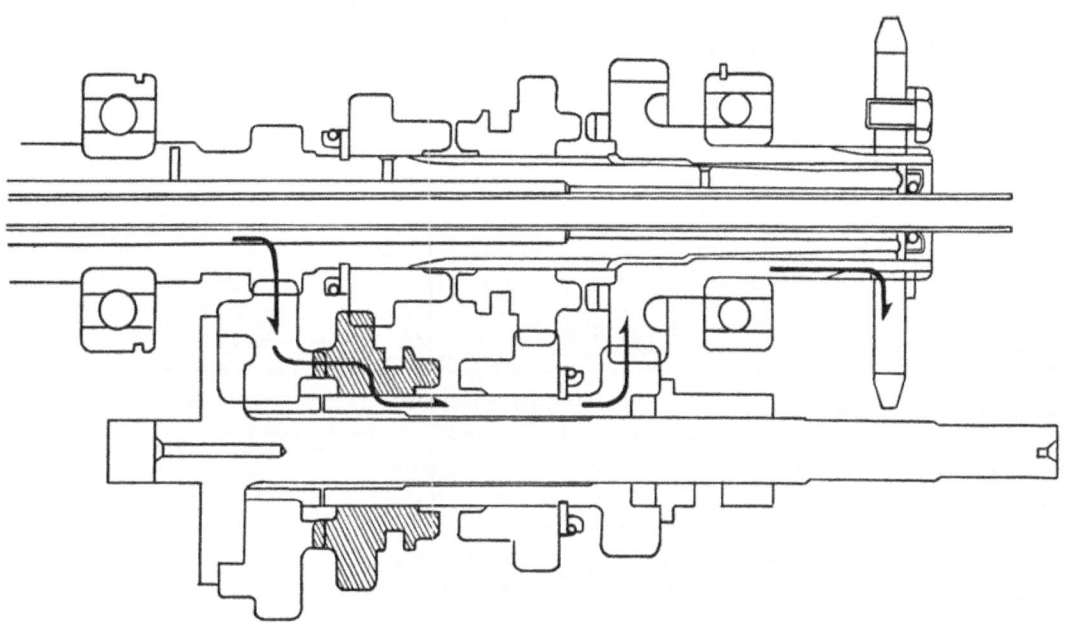

Fig. 3-6. The first

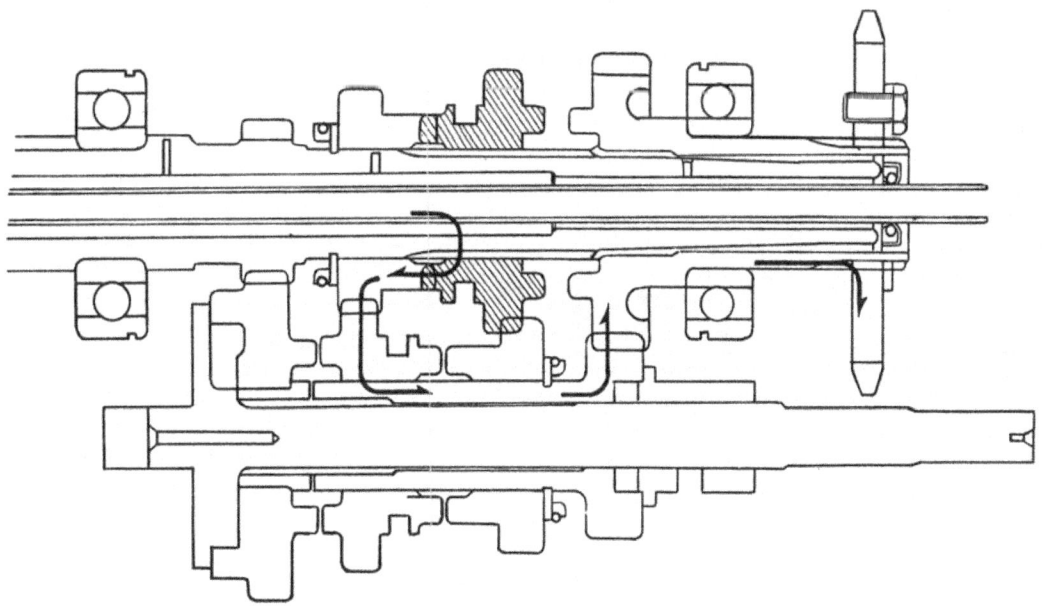

Fig. 3-7. The second

Explaining in order, from the crank rotation is transmitted to the clutch, and the mission shaft is rotated to turn the low gear (7). The low gear turns sliding over the kick-starter spindle (19). As the counter shaft 2 gear (9) which .is connected with the spline on the counter shaft complete can move freely axially, move this to the left side by gear shift fork to mate with low gear (Fig. 3-6) then the low gear combines with the counter shaft as one body to transmit power to the top gear (12). Here the axial movement of main shaft gear is restricted by the gear cotter (14) and the set ring (15) but not restricted rotationally. (similarly counter shaft 3 gear (11).)

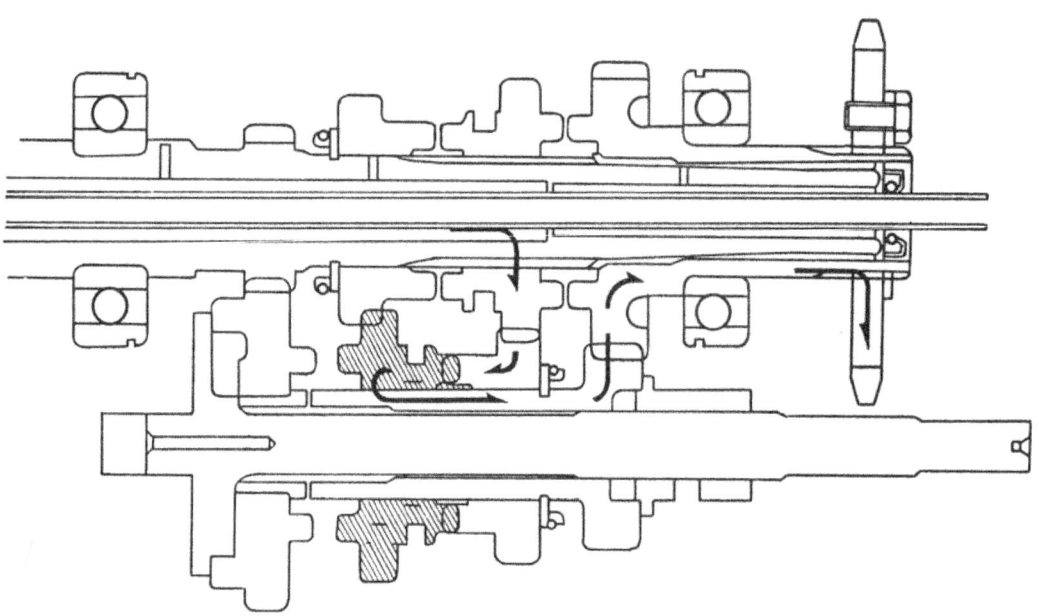

Fig. 3-8. The third

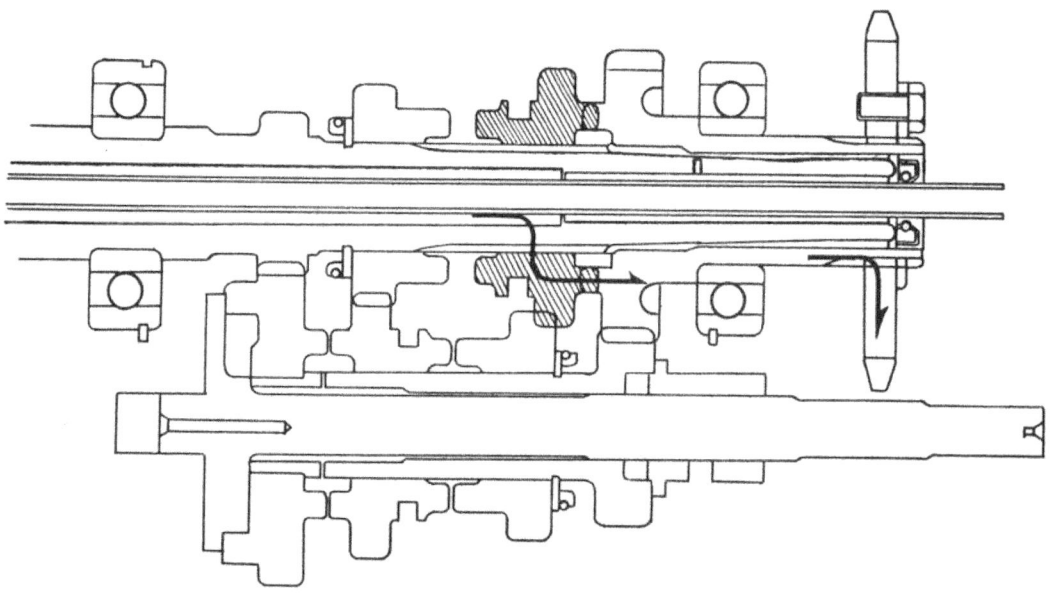

Fig. 3-9. The fourth (Top)

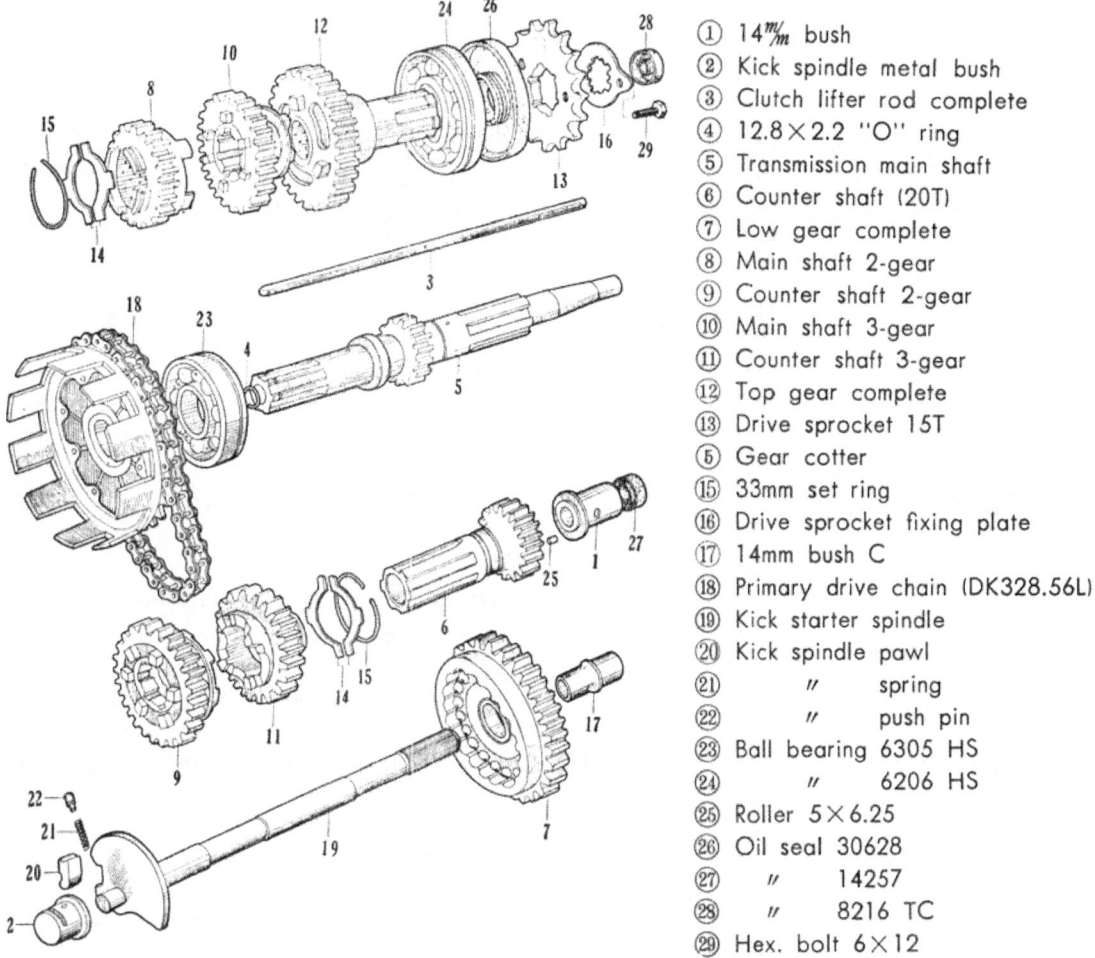

1. 14 m/m bush
2. Kick spindle metal bush
3. Clutch lifter rod complete
4. 12.8 × 2.2 "O" ring
5. Transmission main shaft
6. Counter shaft (20T)
7. Low gear complete
8. Main shaft 2-gear
9. Counter shaft 2-gear
10. Main shaft 3-gear
11. Counter shaft 3-gear
12. Top gear complete
13. Drive sprocket 15T
14. Gear cotter
15. 33mm set ring
16. Drive sprocket fixing plate
17. 14mm bush C
18. Primary drive chain (DK328.56L)
19. Kick starter spindle
20. Kick spindle pawl
21. 〃 spring
22. 〃 push pin
23. Ball bearing 6305 HS
24. 〃 6206 HS
25. Roller 5 × 6.25
26. Oil seal 30628
27. 〃 14257
28. 〃 8216 TC
29. Hex. bolt 6 × 12

Fig. 3-10.

Similarly for the second, protrusion of main shaft 3 gear (10) combine with that of mainshaft 2-gear (8) by actuating another shift fork, and power is transmitted by rotating mainshaft 2-gear (8) connected by protrusion with mainshaft 3-gear (10) mounted on the spline of mainshaft transmitting to countergear (3) and by spline from counter shaft to the top gear.

As for the third, protrusion of counter shaft 2 gear (9) combine with that of counter shaft 3 gear (11) to transmit power to the top gear (12) through counter shaft (6). And for the Top, mainshaft 3 gear (10) combine with the protrusion of the top gear and rotation of mainshaft is transmitted straightly to the drive sprocket to drive the drive-chain. As for the neutral, each protrusion is not combined so power is not transfer to the top gear.

Besides, there is equipped a switch to indicate neutral state, which put light on a indicator lamp when the rotary switch combined on the shift drum is in neutral state. The shift mechanism to actuate the above mentioned counter shaft 2 gear and the

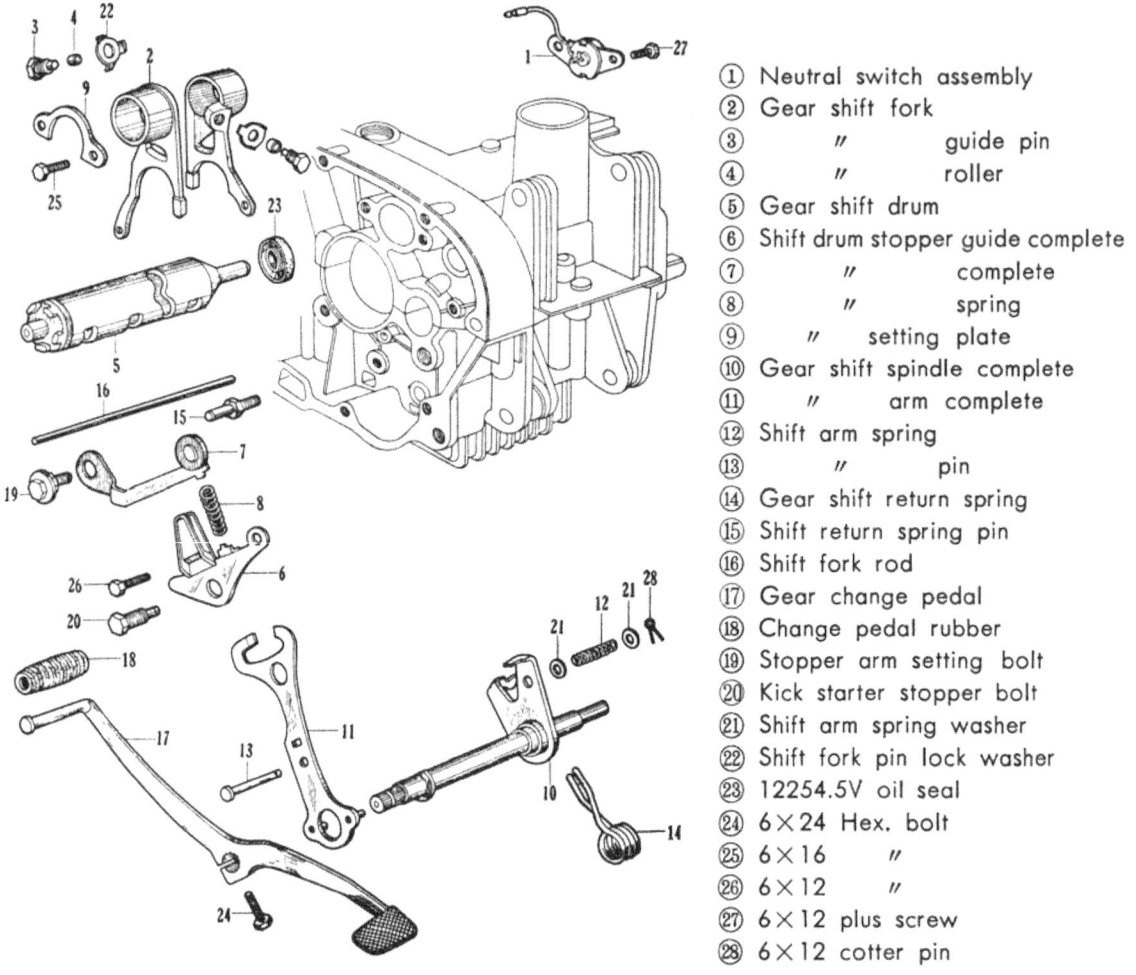

1. Neutral switch assembly
2. Gear shift fork
3. ″   guide pin
4. ″   roller
5. Gear shift drum
6. Shift drum stopper guide complete
7. ″   complete
8. ″   spring
9. ″   setting plate
10. Gear shift spindle complete
11. ″   arm complete
12. Shift arm spring
13. ″   pin
14. Gear shift return spring
15. Shift return spring pin
16. Shift fork rod
17. Gear change pedal
18. Change pedal rubber
19. Stopper arm setting bolt
20. Kick starter stopper bolt
21. Shift arm spring washer
22. Shift fork pin lock washer
23. 12254.5V oil seal
24. 6×24 Hex. bolt
25. 6×16   ″
26. 6×12   ″
27. 6×12 plus screw
28. 6×12 cotter pin

Fig. 3-11.

main shaft 3 gear is explained as follows. In Fig. 3-11 when the gear change pedal (17) is pushed down, the gear shift spindle (10) is turned, and consequently the gear shift arm (11) will turn the drum (5) being pushed by the protrusion on the left end of this gear shift drum.

As there are shift fork guide pin (3) and guide pin roller (4) which fitted on the gear shift fork (2) in the groove on the center part of the shift drum, rotation of drum actuates gear shift fork to move along the form of the groove from side to side and the shift gear is actuated. Here gear shift return spring (14) is fitted to return the change pedal to original position and prepare next action and shift drum stopper (6) is guide (7) for it.

Other parts of the kick starter system are kick spindle pawl (20) and kick spindle pawl spring (21). This pawl mates with the inside groove of the low gear to rotate low gear. When not kicked, the head part of this pawl is pushed by protruded part inside crank case, and pawl is pulled in to free the gear.

C. Final drive mechanism

The drive mechanism from crank to the rear wheel is called final drive mechanism. The main parts are as shown in Figure, primary reduction (intermediate reduction), clutch, mission, final drive (propeller shaft, final reduction) wheel and tyre.

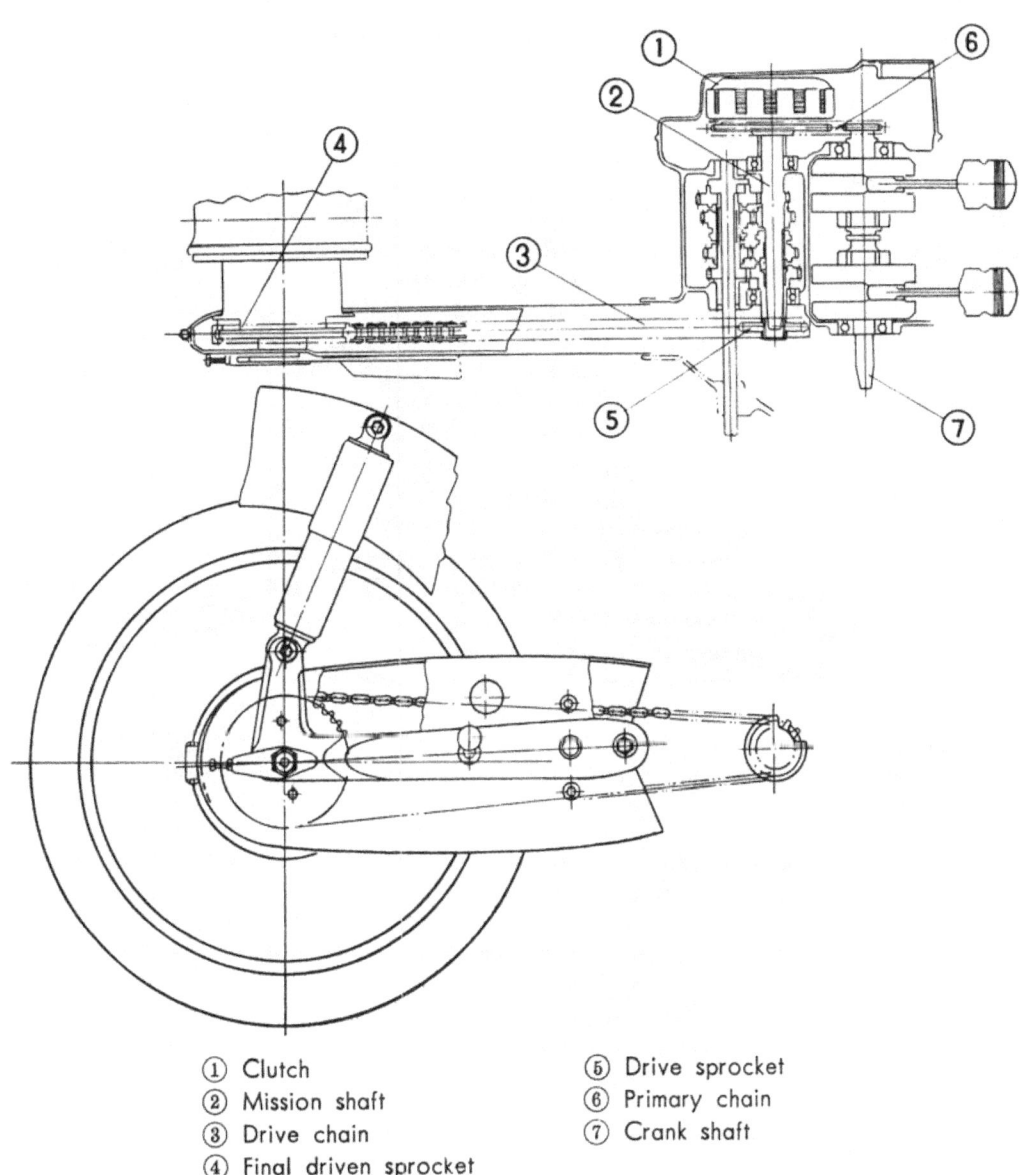

① Clutch
② Mission shaft
③ Drive chain
④ Final driven sprocket
⑤ Drive sprocket
⑥ Primary chain
⑦ Crank shaft

Fig. 3-12.

4. AUXILIARY PARTS

A. Funnel type breather

Breather chamber of funnel type is located on the rear upper side of the upper crank case. Inside the chamber breather body is supported by a spring and back pressure is guided along the direction as shown in the Figure separating oil to outside of crank case. Here a check valve is fitted to avoid outside vapour to be sucked.

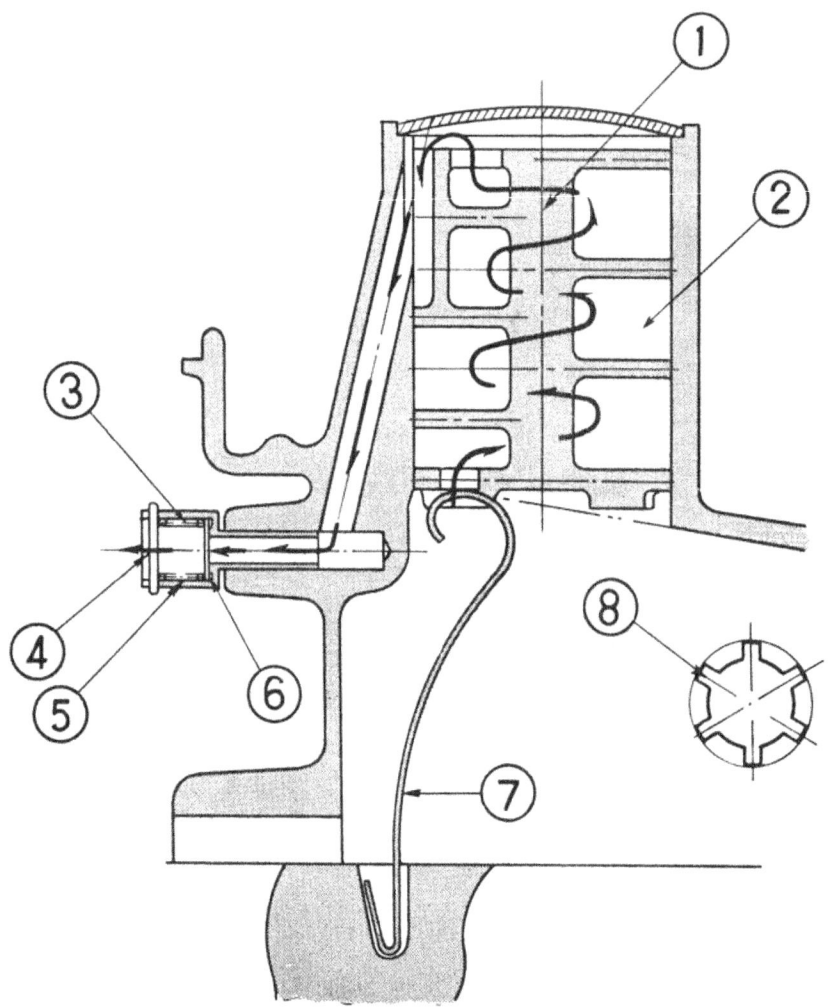

① Breather body
② Breather chamber
③ Breather valve spring
④ Cotter pin
⑤ Breather valve body
⑥ Breather valve
⑦ Breather support spring
⑧ Breather valve (plain view)

Fig. 4-1.

B. Kick starter mechanism

Kick spindle pawl for Model C72, 77 mates with the inside groove of low gear by pawl spring to rotate low gear. When not in kick, the head of pawl is pressed down by kick spindle metal bush so that low gear attains free state.

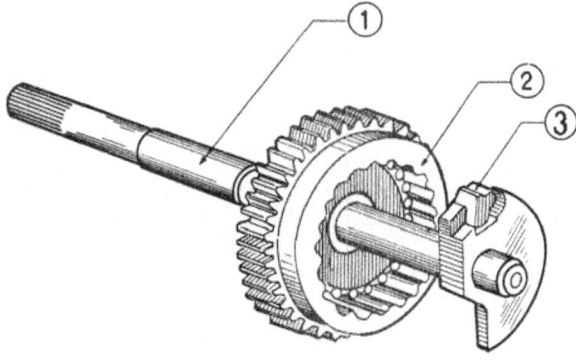

① Kick starter spin
② Low gear complete
③ Kick spindle panel

Fig. 4-2.

For Model CB72, 77, considering relation with the chassis, advance step kick system was applied. A piece of gear was set inside the R crank case cover to reverse direction of rotation and can start engine transmitting rotational power to the kick spindle pawl. (Fig. 4-3)

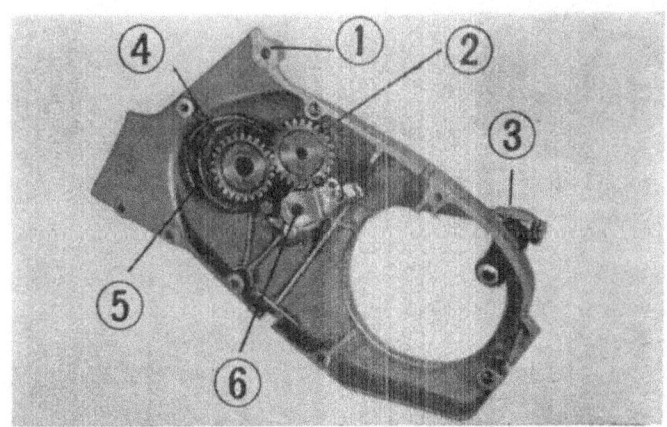

① R. crank case cover comp.
② Kick starter gear
③ Kick arm
④ Kick starter pinion
⑤ Kick starter spring
⑥ Clutch lifter thread comp.

Fig. 4-3. Crank case cover

C. Cam chain tensioner

Inside cam chain chamber located at center part of cylinder cam chain (DK219-94L) is set to transmit rotational motion of crank to cam shaft, and cam chain tension is applied to make high speed motion of cam chain correctly and smoothly. Here the cam chain tension works to supress waving of chain by pressing cam chain. In Figure 4-4, 6mm bolt fitted on the tensioner push bar be loosen, the roller will be pushed out by a spring to give a adequate tension on the chain. According to slackness of chain adjustment can be done by this set screw. To make sure tightness of chain, it is favorable to adjust putting the crank shaft at the lower dead point.

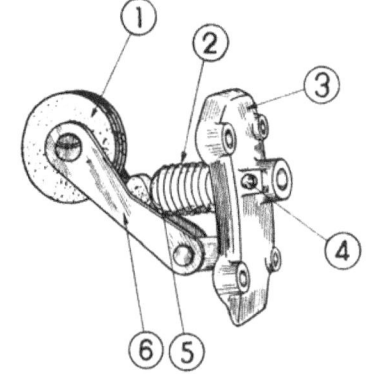

① Cam chain tensioner
② Cam chain tensioner spring
③ Tensioner holder
④ 6mm bolt
⑤ Cam chain tensioner push bar
⑥ Cam chain tensioner arm

Fig. 4-4.

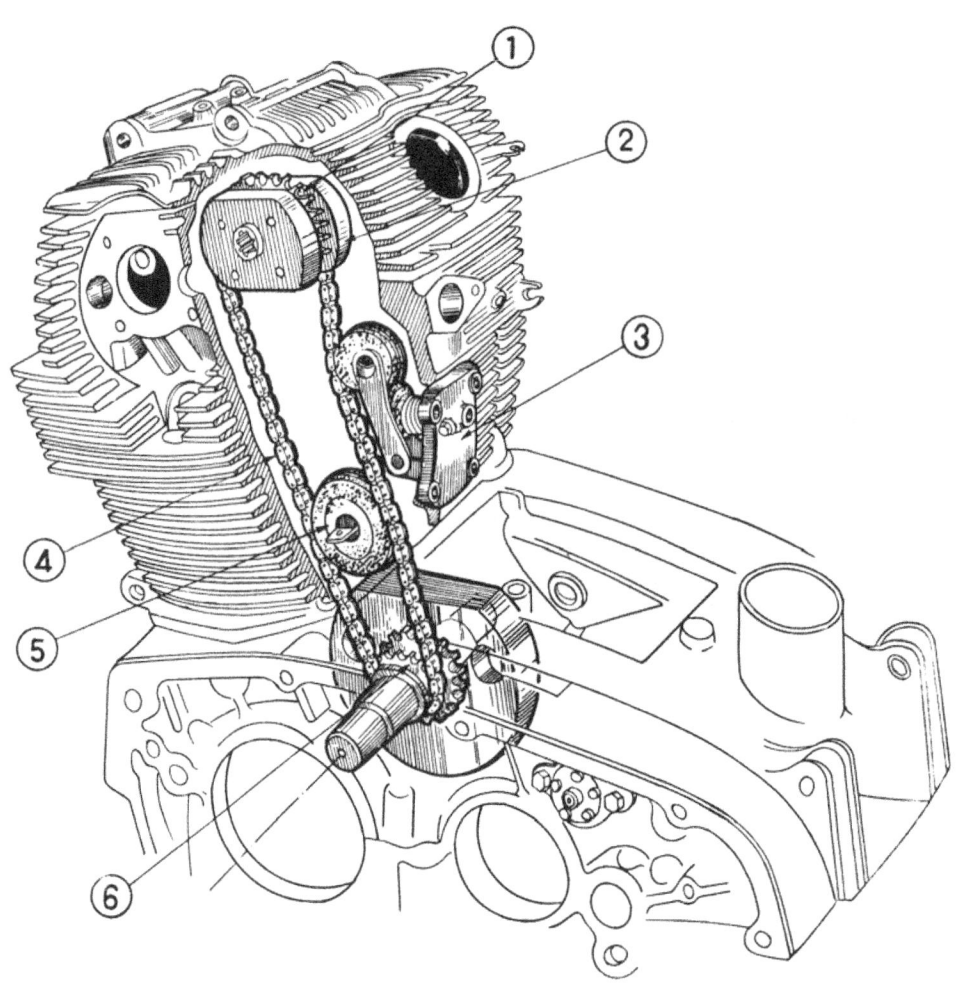

① Cam sprocket
② R cam shaft fly wheel
③ Cam chain tensioner
④ Cam chain
⑤ Cam chain guide roller
⑥ Center crank shaft

Fig. 4-5.

5. CARBURETTOR

The carburetor is a device for supplying fuel and air into the engine. The performance of the carburetor will depend upon such factors as most suitable mixture proportion of atomized fuel under all conditions of speed and load of the engine. Therefore it must has precision for each part and high resistance for wear to assure the reliable performance for a long period, and so it is required inspection and maintenance.

The revised parts of Model C72 from Model C71 are as follow.

(1) Elimination of manifold.
(2) Fitting type Down Draft type.
(3) Addition of power jet.

Comparing Model CB72, 77 with Model C72, 77 2-carburettor system was adopted to increase Horse power by eliminating branch to suction post. Concerning the power jet mentioned above, when MJイ# is set, the best condition is at 4000 rpm, and at 8000 rpm mixture becomes thin, but when MJロ# is set at 8000 rpm the best and at 4000 rpm becomes rich.

Therefore to get favorable condition between 4000 rpm and 8000 rpm, MJイ# was selected to apply the power jet from 6000 rpm to meet high rotation developing performance at medium and high power.

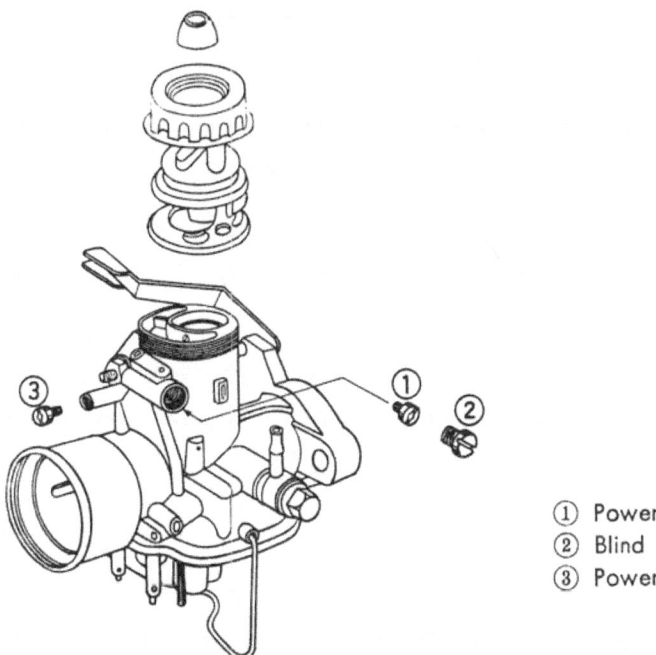

① Power jet
② Blind plug
③ Power air jet

Fig. 5-1. Power jet system

Construction

(1) Air from the air cleaner passes through the suction port (1), lower side of the throttle valve (6), main bore (8) and into the cylinders.

This air stream produces a partial vacuum in the area around the power nozzle (24), by which fuel in the float chamber (2) flows through power jet fuel pipe (23), power jet (22) to the power nozzle (24). At this area, fuel is mixed with air introduced through the power air jet (21). Then they are mixed with air flowing from the suction port, vaporized and drawn into the cylinder (Fig. 5-2).

(2) Main Fuel system.

Air from the air cleaner passes through the suction port (1), lower side of the throttle valve (6) main bore (8) and into the cylinders. This air stream produces a partial vacuum in the area around the needle jet (4), by which fuel in the float chamber (2) flows through the main jet (10) into the needle jet holder (3). As this area, fuel is mixed with air (bleed air) introduced through the air jet (5) and the holes (9) provided around the needle jet holder (3). Then fuel and air travel the gap between the needle jet (4) and the jet needle (7), and discharge to the lower side of the throttle valve. Then they are mixed with air flowing from the suction port, vaporized and drawn into the cylinder (Fig. 5-2).

(3) Slow speed fuel system (pilot system).

Air from the suction port (1) passes through the outside (12) of the air screw (11) which regulates the rate of air flow. Then air passes through the bleed holes (14) of the slow speed jet (13) to the slow speed jet (13) where introduced into fuel stream from the orifice (15) provided with the bottom of the slow speed jet (13). The rich mixture produced at this area discharges to the lower side of the throttle valve and is mixed with air flowing from the suction port (1) and drawn into the cylinder. The minor mixture adjustment is made by means of the air screw (11). Turn the air screw to the right to enrich the mixture and to the left to lean the mixture. The major mixture adjustment is made by replacing the slow speed jet (13). Replace the jet with one carrying bigger number to enrich the mixture and with one carrying smaller number to lean the mixture (Fig. 5-2).

(4) Float chamber

The carburetor must supply the correct mixtures which suit to the throttle opening and the engine running speed. In this connection, the fuel level must be held constant. The float system is a device to maintain this constant height. The operation of the float system is given in the following. Fuel from the tank enters the float chamber

(2) through the passage (16), the valve seat (17) and valve (18). As fuel enters the float chamber, the float (19) will raise and move the valve (18) upperward by means of the float arm (20). When the valve touches the valve seat, flow of fuel will be restricted. As fuel level drops, the float lowers, opening the valve to allow fuel to enter the float chamber. Thus, any change in the fuel level causes a corresponding movement of the float, opening or closing the valve to maintain the fuel level constant. There is a spring installed, against vibration, between the needle valve and its body at the location where the valve contracts the float arm (20). (Fig. 5-2).

(5) Choke system

The choke valve (21) must be in a closed position with the choke lever moved upwards, and in a open position with the choke lever moved downward, as shown in Fig. 5-2.

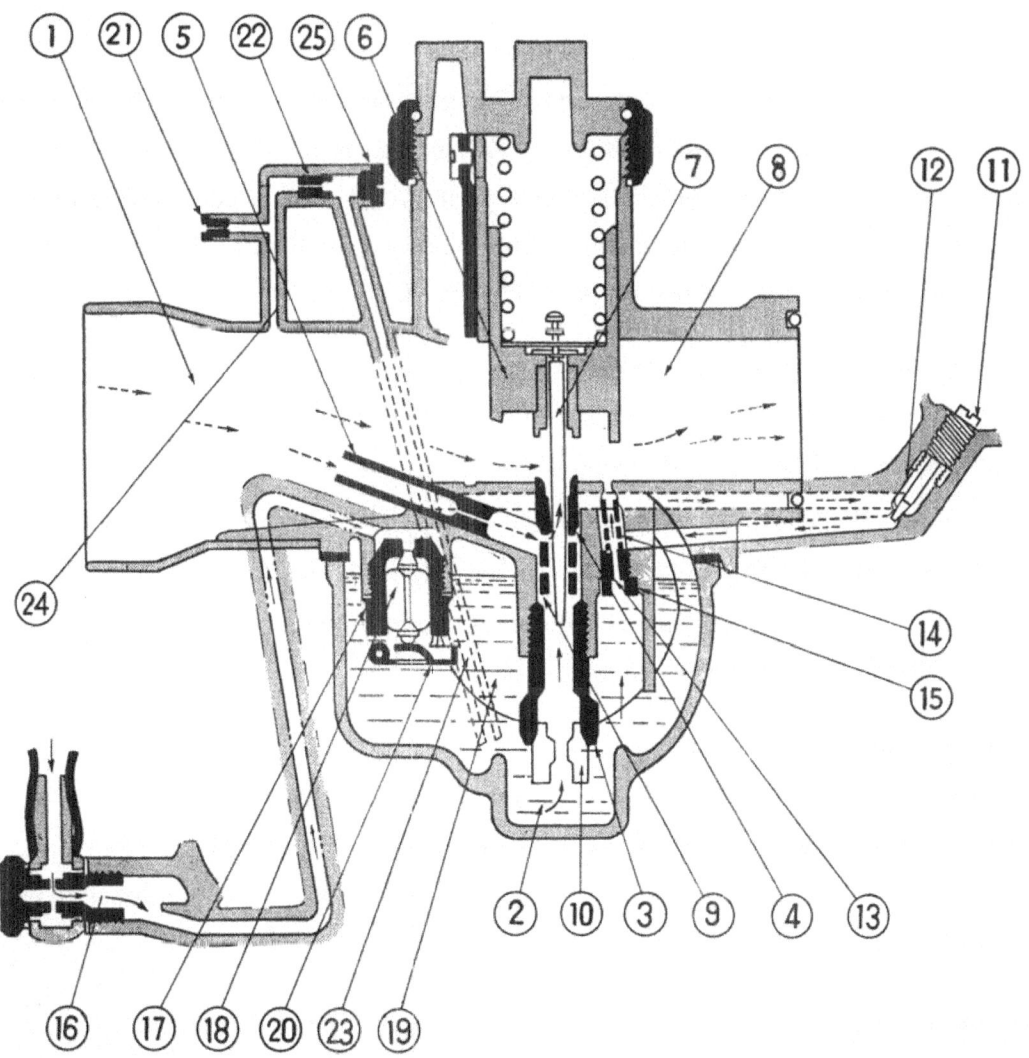

Fig. 5-2.

(6) Adjustment

    a) High speed Fuel mixture adjustment

        Fuel mixture between full and half open throttle positions is controlled by the main jet. To determine whether the main jet is correct, slightly close the choke valve with the engine running at full throttle.

        1. If the engine speed increases, the fuel mixture is too lean.

        2. If the engine speed decreases, the main jet in correct or too big.

        Replace the main jet as necessary in such cases.

    b) Moderate speed Fuel mixture adjustment.

        Fuel mixture between half and one eighth throttle positions is controlled by the adjustable jet needle and cut away of throttle valve.

        1. If the muffler is black smoking, the mixture is too rich. Lower the jet needle to the next lower position.

        2. If the engine misfires or hesitates when accelerated or driven at moderate speed, the mixture is too lean. Raise the jet needle to the next upper position.

        The throttle valve cut away carrying larger number bring the mixture leaner while one carrying smaller number bring the mixture richer. Since the change on the cutaway affects the engine performance below one eighth throttle position, the replacement of the throttle valve should be done carefully.

    c) Low speed Fuel mixture adjustment.

        Fuel mixture between one eighth and idle throttle positions is controlled by the air screw and throttle cut away.

        1. Adjustment must be done by the air screw mostly. Turn the air screw "in" to enrich the mixture and "Out" to lean the mixture.

        2. If the correct adjustment cannot be obtained by the turning of air screw, replace the throttle valve.

(7) Fuel level adjustment

As shown in Fig. 5-3, fuel level is determined by the height H measured from the bottom of main bore, which varies among each different engines. However, since the fuel level cannot be measured easily, it is recommended to determine by height h, of the float.

Float adjustment

    a) Place the carbureter upside down.

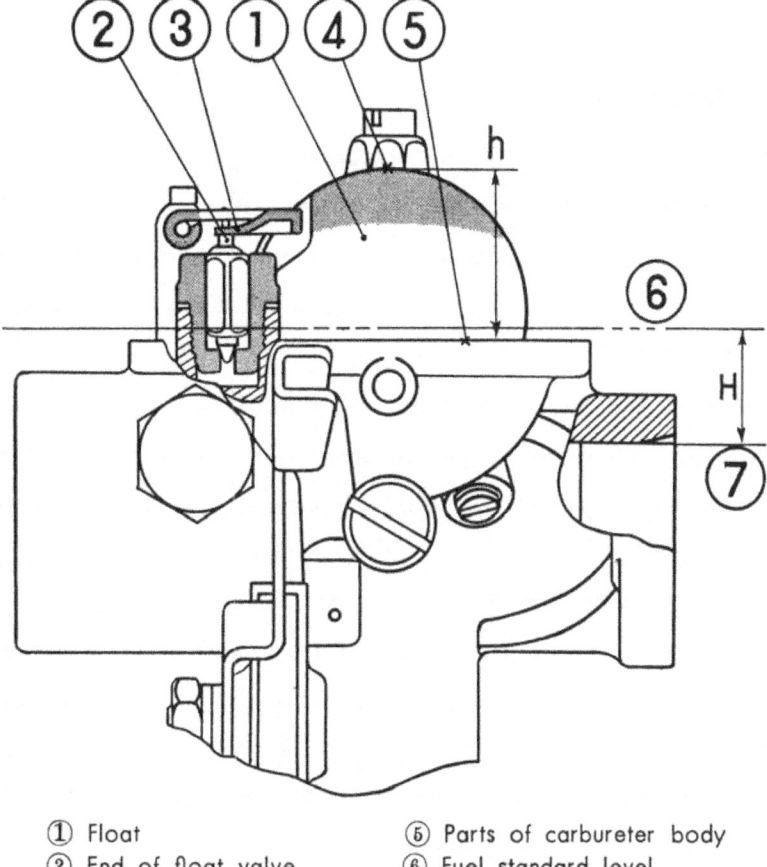

① Float
② End of float valve
③ Float arm
④ End of float
⑤ Parts of carbureter body
⑥ Fuel standard level
⑦ Main bore bottom line

Fig. 5-3. Measurement of fuel standard level

b) When the float is supported with fingers, find the position where the float arm is about to touch the top of the float valve or the position having clearance of 0.1mm.

c) At this position height difference between the end of float and the carbureter body should equal to h and if it is more or less than this amount, adjust the height, raising or bending the float arm carefully.

       h of Pw 22   26.5 mm
       h of Pw 26   22.5 mm

[Note]

At the tip of the float valve there is inserted a spring which creeps inside when pushed. As it prevent to show the actual position where the valve is to be closed, it is necessary to be cautious to see the contact point between the float arm and float valve.

6. FRAME

Construction of frame body

The frame supporting engine contacts with ground through the front and rear wheels and is the skelton of whole chassis. Further it has important feature affecting its form and design. The main function of frame is to maintain chassis strength, supporting engine, rider, and load on the carrier, and has to endure shock due to roughness of road through tyre and shock absorber.

On the other hand it requires rigidity from viewpoints of controlability, and further requires light weight to attain better running performance. The frame body of Honda 250 · 300 Model C72, 77 is, made of steel of stress skin construction and adopted such cross sectional form as refregerator having round corner. The type of form has high strength to bending moment and torsion. Therefore this would be most favorable form of construction for motor cycle frame having high rigidity from manufacturing viewpoints.

Especially welding is done by new type of seam welder to attain reliable connection and also uniform products having beautiful outlook. On the other hand for the frame of Model CB72, 77, as main strength members, high carbon steel tubings were adopted to attain light weight and to increase rigidity.

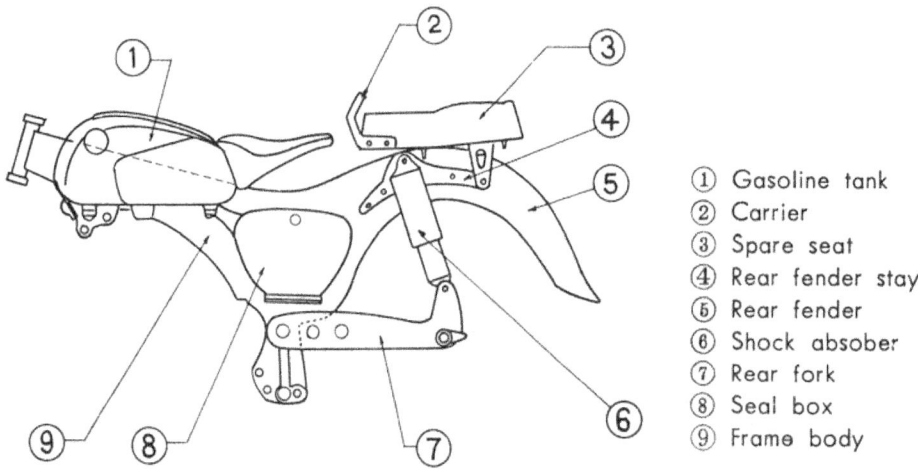

① Gasoline tank
② Carrier
③ Spare seat
④ Rear fender stay
⑤ Rear fender
⑥ Shock absober
⑦ Rear fork
⑧ Seal box
⑨ Frame body

Fig. 6-1. Frame body for Model C72, 77.

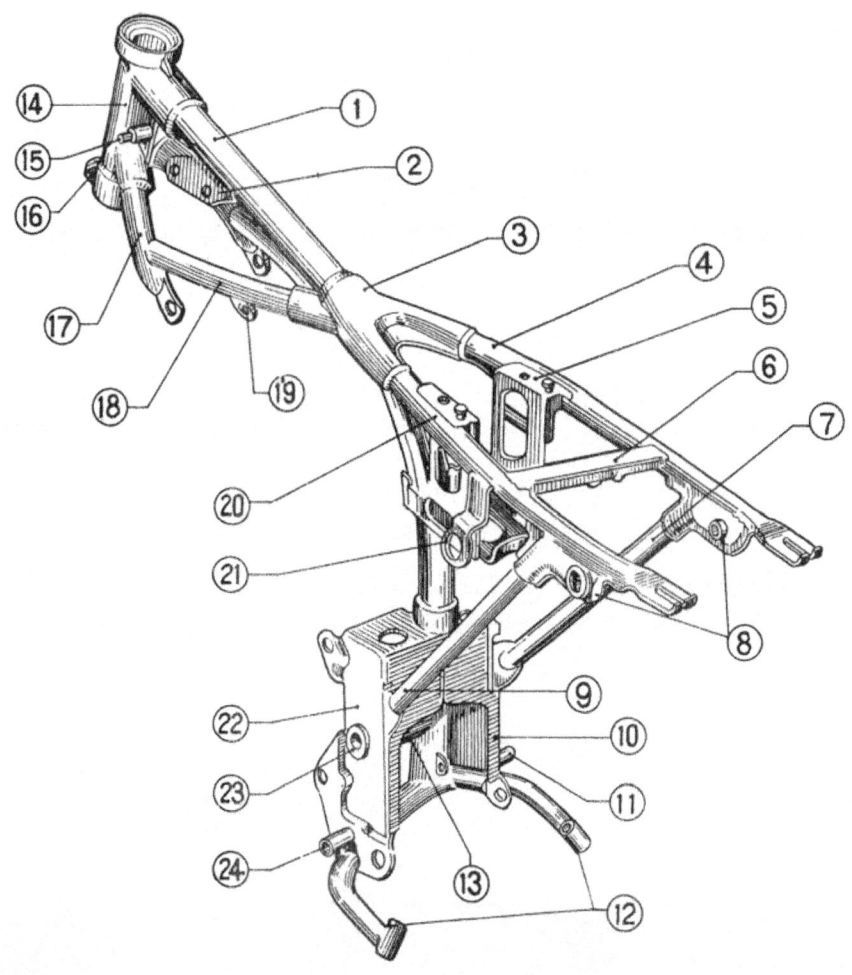

① Main pipe
② Coil setting plate
③ Tube holder
④ R. sub-tube
⑤ Battery support Stay
⑥ Sub-tube cross-member
⑦ R. sub-tube holder
⑧ R.L. rear cushion upper bracket
⑨ L. sub-tube holder
⑩ R. bottom plate
⑪ R. step holder piece
⑫ Muffler setting pipe
⑬ Center pipe
⑭ Steering head pipe
⑮ Fuel tank holder
⑯ Key hole
⑰ Front down tube
⑱ Drivers tube
⑲ Engine hanger plate
⑳ L. sub-tube
㉑ Main switch bracket
㉒ L. bottom plate
㉓ Center pipe bushing
㉔ L. step holder piece

Fig. 6-2. Frame body for CB72, 77.

7. SUSPENSION

A. Front wheel suspension

The front fork of Model C72, 77 is made of pressed steel and for Model CB72, 77 telescopic fork was adopted to increase rigidity and to attain better running stability on rough road. As the cushion, the link system made it possible to reduce wheel base variation and to attain better feeling on riding and better controllability.

As shown in the Figure of shock absorber, it consists of the main spring and Double cylindrical oil dumper. The spring takes up compression load and the damper takes up recoiling force.

For Model C72, 77, left and right front cushions are combined by the suspension arm as one body, but for Model CB72, 77 there is no suspension arm. In the oil damper of Model CB72, 77 there contains white spindle oil 200 cc, and maximum stroke is 80 mm.

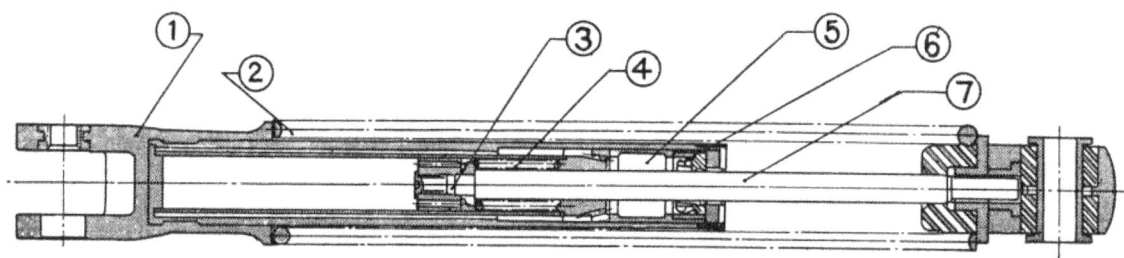

① Front cushion bottom metal comp.
② Front cushion spring front damper inner pipe
③ Front damper piston
④ Front cushion bebound stopper spring
⑤ Front damper collar
⑥ Front damper oil seal
⑦ Front damper rod

Fig. 7-1. Cross-section of Front cushion for Model C72, 77.

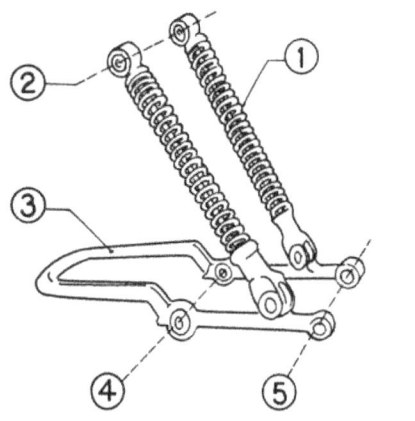

① Front cushion
② Hinge
③ Suspension arm
④ Supporting hinge
⑤ Wheel axis

Fig. 7-2.

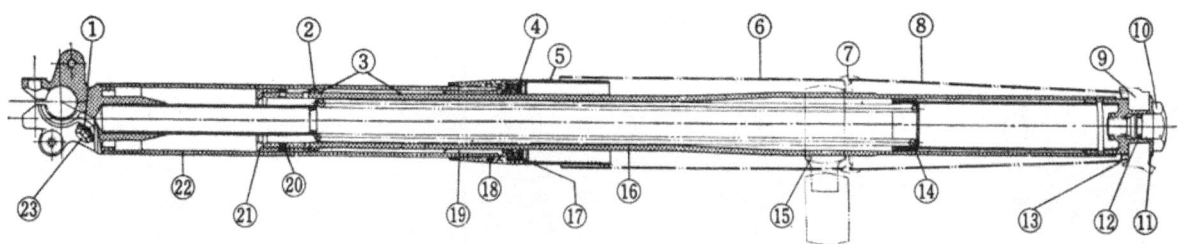

① Fork drain cock packing
② Front damper valve
③ Fork pipe stopper ring
④ 334610, oil seal
⑤ Front fork seal housing
⑥ Front fork upper cover
⑦ Front fork rib
⑧ Front fork upper cover
⑨ Fork top bridge
⑩ Front fork bolt
⑪ Front fork washer
⑫ "O" ring, 9.4×2.4
⑬ Front fork cover packing
⑭ Front cushion spring
⑮ Fork bottom bridge
⑯ Front fork pipe comp.
⑰ Front fork oil seal retainer
⑱ Ring, 40.5×3.0
⑲ Front fork pipe guide
⑳ Fork piston knock pin
㉑ Front fork piston
㉒ Front fork bottom case
㉓ Front fork drain cock bolt

Fig. 7-3. Cross section of Front cushion of Model CB72, 77.

B. Rear wheel suspension

The rear wheel is pivot type construction equipped with also shock absorber. The principle of construction of the shock absorber is alike that of the front wheel excepting such point as side pressure don't act on the sliding part and construction of orifice on the absorber is different. Special attention was paid on the suspension system on the pivot side as performance of shock absorber, manufacturing around the pivot and rigidity of rear fork affect on feeling of riding greatly.

As the rear fork of Model CB72, 77, main strength members was made of high carbon steel tubing to attain light weight and to raise rigidity.

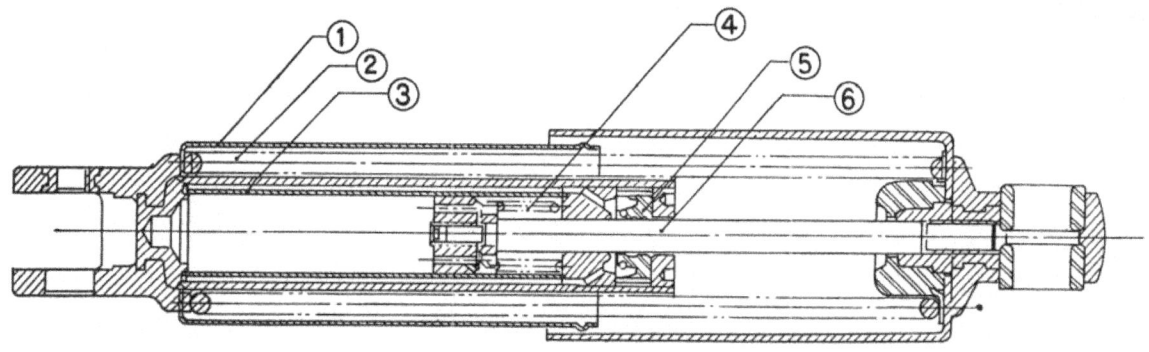

① Rear cushion metal comp.
② Rear cushion spring
③ Rear damper inner-pipe
④ Rear rebound stopper spring
⑤ Rear damper oil seal
⑥ Rear damper rod.

Fig. 7-4. Cross-section of rear cushion of Model C72.

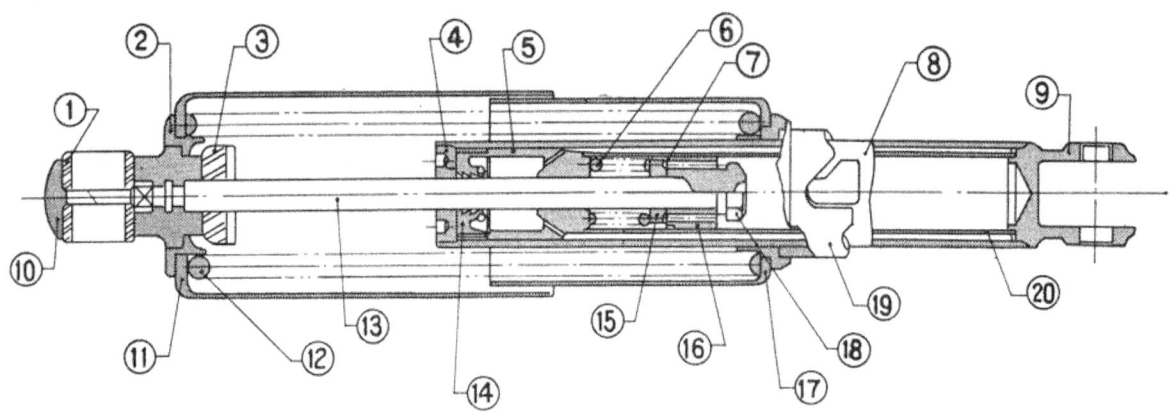

① Rear cushion rubber bushing
② Rear cushion spring seat
③ Rear cushion stopper
④ Rear damper nut
⑤ Rear damper rod guide
⑥ Rear Cushion rebound stopper spring
⑦ Rear damper valve
⑧ Rear damper case comp.
⑨ Rear damper under joint
⑩ Rear cushion upper joint
⑪ Rear cushion upper case
⑫ Rear cushion spring
⑬ Rear damper rod
⑭ Rear damper oil seal
⑮ Rear damper valve stopper
⑯ Rear damper piston
⑰ Rear cushion bottom case
⑱ Rear damper piston nut
⑲ Rear cushion spring adjuster
⑳ Rear damper inner-pipe

Fig. 7-5. Cross-section of rear cushion of Model CB72, 77.

In the cylinder of the rear cushion there contains 60# spindle oil 37 cc for Model C72, 77 and 47 cc for Model CB72, 77. When the rear wheel got shock rear cushion spring is compressed to absorb it and rebounding force is restricted by the oil damper to give adequate cushioning.

If the amount of oil contained in the damper is not suitable, effective stroke of cushion becomes to short or leaks oil or sometimes become origin of shock sound. The rear cushion of Model CB72, 77 is designed to enable three steps of adjustment according to road condition and running state.

MEMO

8. STEERING SYSTEM

A. Steering handle

Special attention was paid in designing the Steering Handle as this affect feeling of riding and easy control.

Especially for Model C72, it was aimed to take riding posture easy to correspond quick manipulation of control, which would be determined by the form of the handle, saddle and step. Moreover on control parts, adjustment equipments are attached according to each riders' choice. These features could be said to symbolize Honda's kindness.

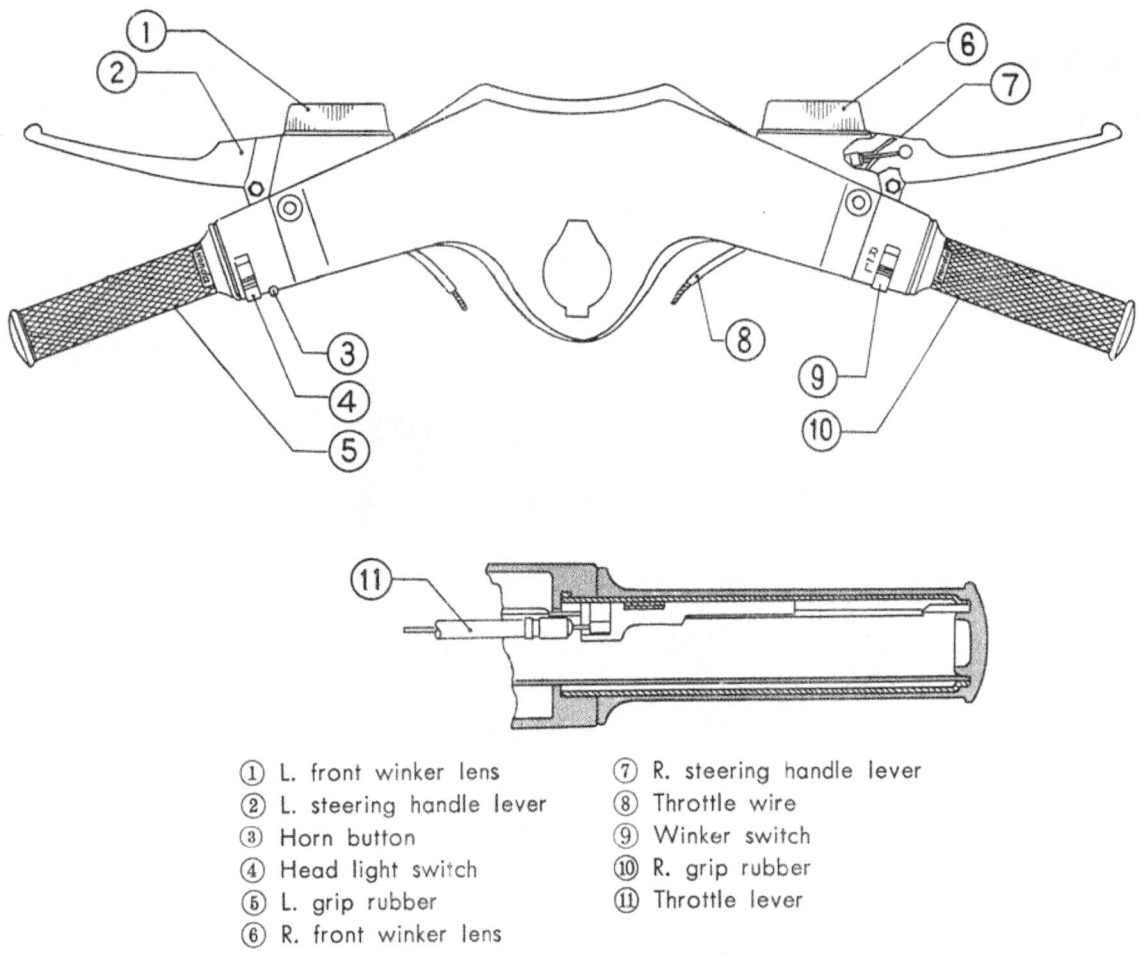

① L. front winker lens
② L. steering handle lever
③ Horn button
④ Head light switch
⑤ L. grip rubber
⑥ R. front winker lens
⑦ R. steering handle lever
⑧ Throttle wire
⑨ Winker switch
⑩ R. grip rubber
⑪ Throttle lever

Fig. 8-1 Handle of Model C72, 77.

The handle complete of Model CB72, 77 is made of one piece of steel tubing attached to the fork top bridge by means of the handle pipe holder. The fork top bridge is fixed on the front cushion by 2 front fork bolts. Each wire is exposed in assembly to make it easy to replace the handle.

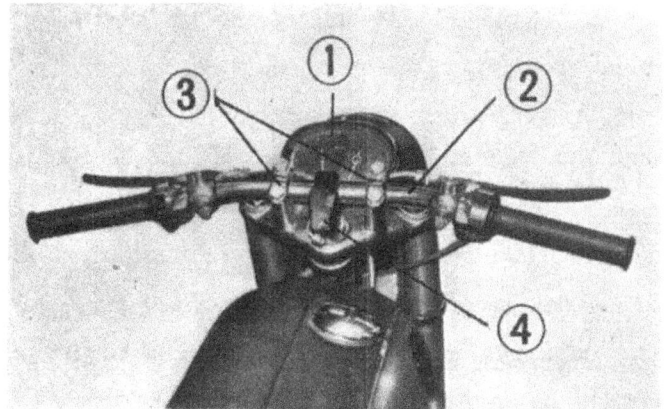

Fig. 8-2. Handle assembly of Model CB72, 77.

① Speedo-Tachometer ass'y
② Steering handle comp.
③ Handle pipe holder
④ Steering damper knob

B. Steering

Construction of steering of Model C72, 77, as shown in the Figure, is such having ball bearing and steering damper of friction plate system to meet requirement from contrallability and stability at low and high speed running.

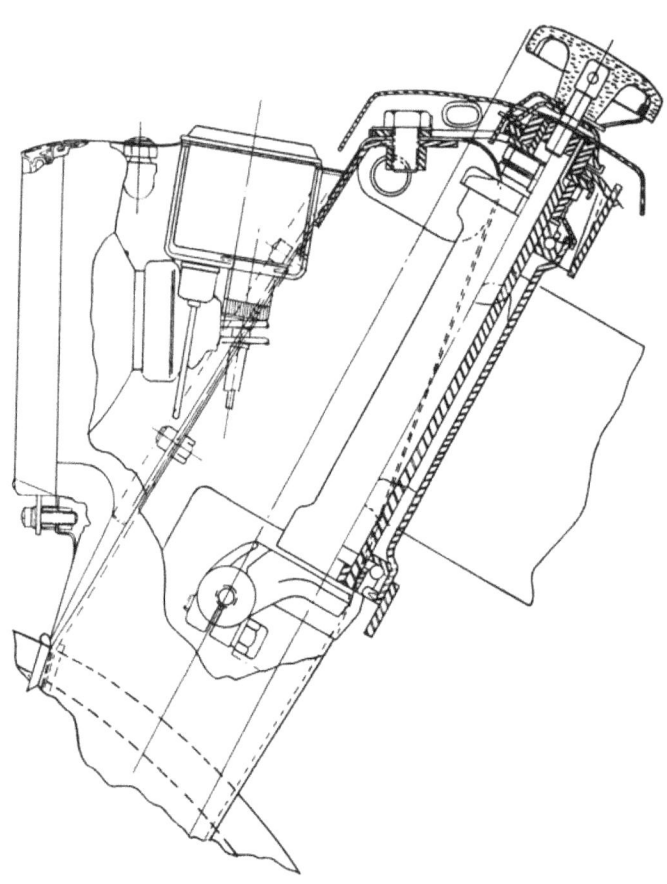

Fig. 8-3. Cross section of steering head of Model C72, 77.

For Model CB72, 77, the steering stem which has cone lathe inside supported on the front cushion by means of 8×32 hexagonal bolt is the rotational axis centering frame head pipe and is important part for steering. On the steering stem, steering damper is attached and can be adjusted according to road condition, running state and loading condition.

If the knob of steering damper be turned to the right, steering damper spring nut is raised upward to cramp steering damper friction disk by means of steering damper plate A and B, consequently handle steering becomes heavy. On the contrary, if the knob be turned to the left, steering damper spring nut is lowered to make gap between plates A and B to become easy steering. (Fig. 8-4)

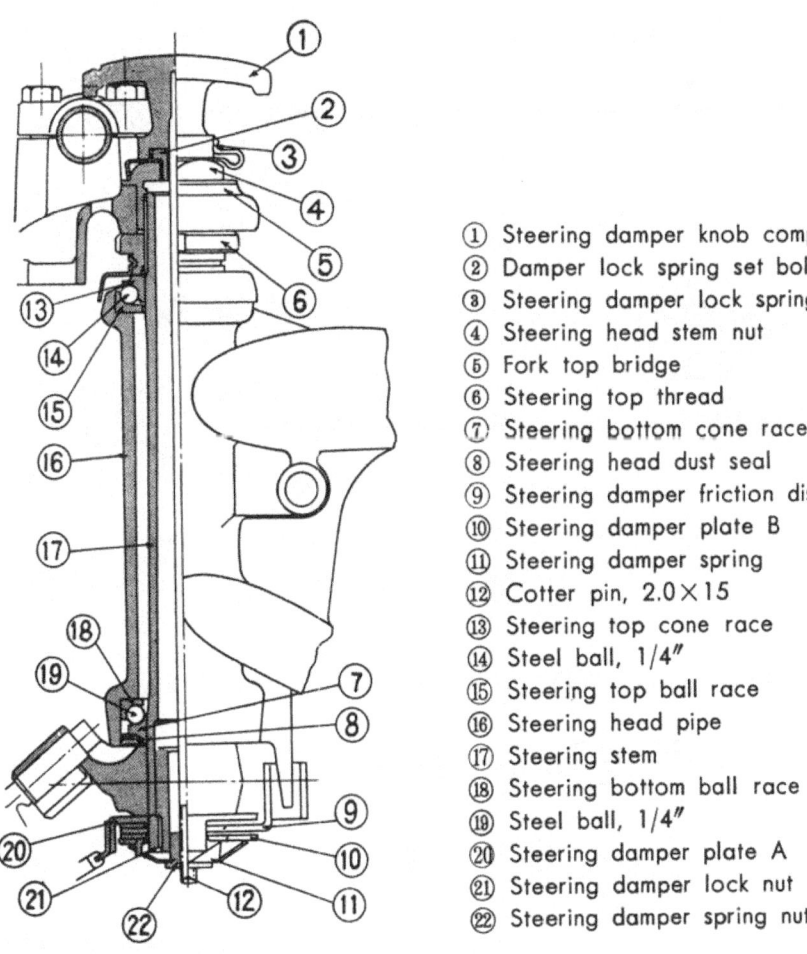

① Steering damper knob comp.
② Damper lock spring set bolt
③ Steering damper lock spring
④ Steering head stem nut
⑤ Fork top bridge
⑥ Steering top thread
⑦ Steering bottom cone race
⑧ Steering head dust seal
⑨ Steering damper friction disk
⑩ Steering damper plate B
⑪ Steering damper spring
⑫ Cotter pin, 2.0×15
⑬ Steering top cone race
⑭ Steel ball, 1/4"
⑮ Steering top ball race
⑯ Steering head pipe
⑰ Steering stem
⑱ Steering bottom ball race
⑲ Steel ball, 1/4"
⑳ Steering damper plate A
㉑ Steering damper lock nut
㉒ Steering damper spring nut

Fig. 8-4. Cross section of steering of Model CB72, 77.

9. BRAKE INSTALLATION

As reliability and durability of Brake installation are indispensable condition for it, manufacturing Brake was paid special attention. Rear wheel braking is done by expanding the brake lining installed is the brake drum which is actuated by link motion to turn the brake cam by pushing right foot.

Here special attention was paid to discipate friction heat generated to get better durability. For the front brake, by right hand operation wire transmits force to work and brake machanism is alike with the rear Installation.

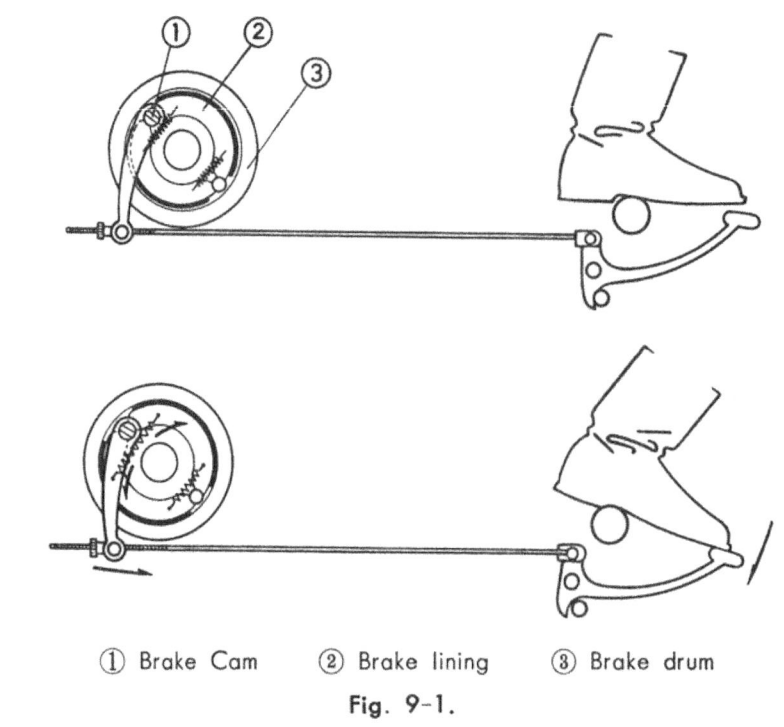

① Brake Cam　② Brake lining　③ Brake drum

Fig. 9-1.

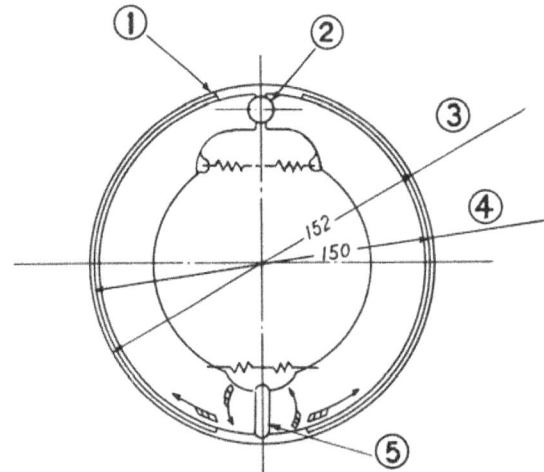

① Brake shoe width 30
② Brake shoe anker pin
③ Brake drum inner dia
④ Brake shoe out dia
⑤ Brake cam

Fig. 9-2

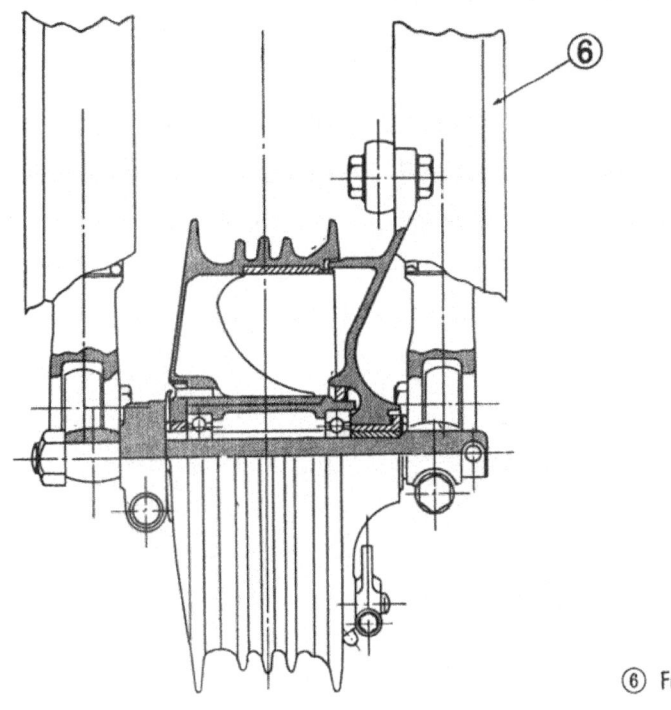

⑥ Front fork

Fig. 9-3.

MEMO

10. CONSTRUCTION OF WHEEL

A. Front wheel

Front wheel body made of aluminium casting of whole width hub containing ball bearings and brake drum inside is fitted with brake panel and speed meter unit by wheel axis and nuts. To assemble the front wheel to the chassis, fit on the lower end of front fork slide pipe by the axle fitting. Reaction occured during braking can be caught by the left side bearing through the stopper of the brake panel.

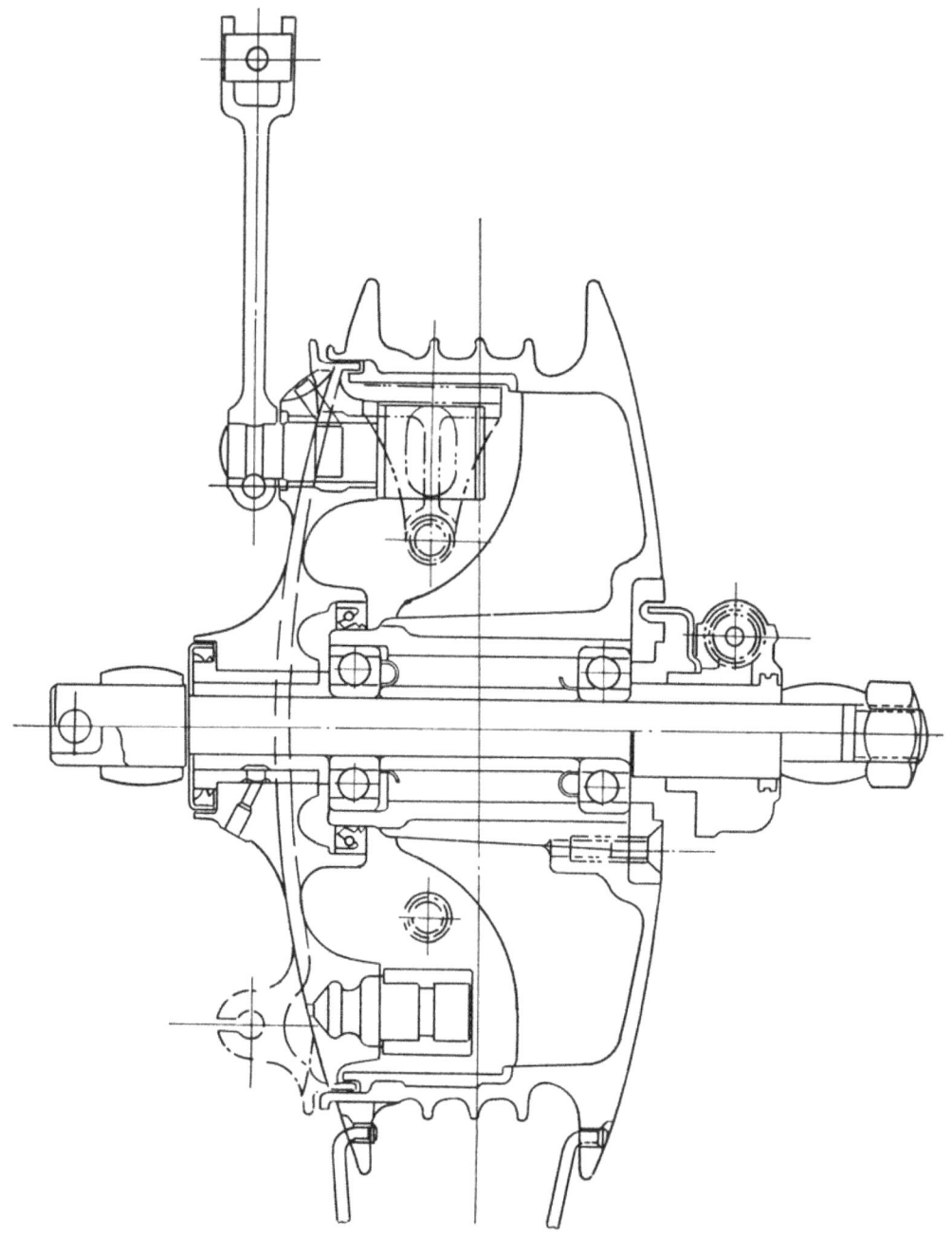

Fig. 10-1. Cross section of front hub.

B. Rear wheel

The rear wheel of Model C72, 77 is consisted of wheel bearing, rear wheel hub of alminium equipped with the brake drum, the final drive flange serving chain case partially and brake panel. On the left side, the brake panel is equipped through the distance collar, and between the wheel hub and the final drive flange there is fitted rear wheel damper.

On the right side of the wheel hub containing ball bearing, the chain case is equipped through the final drive flange fitted with the rear wheel damper and the final driven sprocket, and is tighten on the rear axle passing through the left side of the rear fork through the distance collar on the left side.

The rear wheel damper absorb not only abrupt variation of rotation during braking and driving force of the rear wheel hub, but also is useful to protect transmission mechanism. The rear wheel of Model CB72, 77 is consisted of ball bearing (6304), the rear wheel hub of alminium casting equipped with the brake drum and the brake panel.

On the left side there equipped the rear brake panel of twin cam type through the panel side collar and on the right side of the wheel hub, hub and the final driven sprocket are fixed by the sprocket setting bolt, and fixed on the rear fork by the rear axle through the rear side collar.

Fig. 10-2. To draw out the rear wheel from the frame (Model CB72, 77)

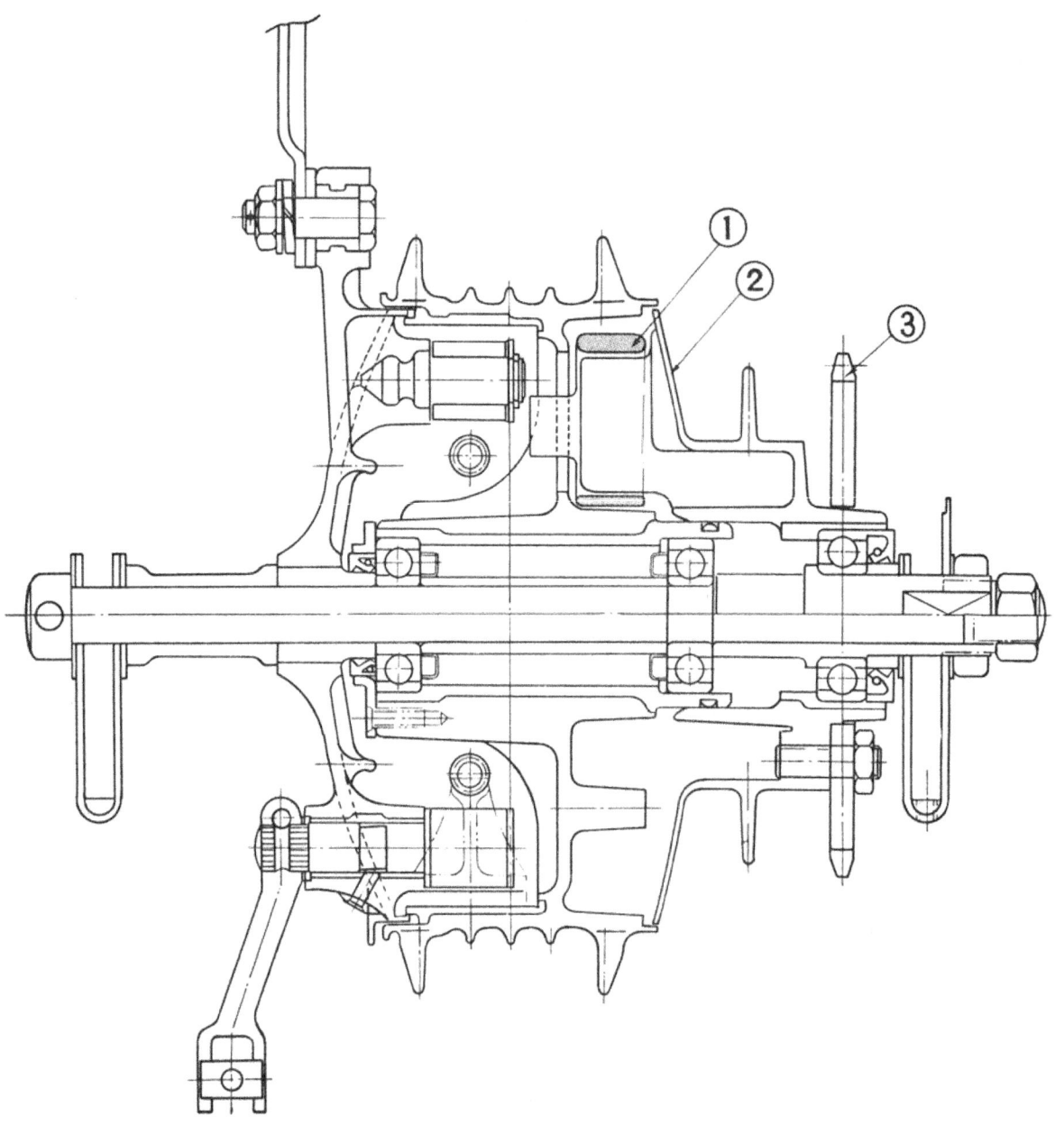

① Rear wheel damper ② Final drive flange ③ Final driven sprocket

Fig. 10-3. Cross section of Rear hub

11. AUXILIARY EQUIPMENT

A. Air cleaner

The Air cleaner element made of filter paper is stored at the center part of the body utilizing a point of excellence that the frame is made of steel sheet. It is aimed to get better filter effect by expanding surface area and also to prevent rain water to enter. For Model CB72, 77, as 2 carbureters are equipped, air cleaners are fixed on both sides each.

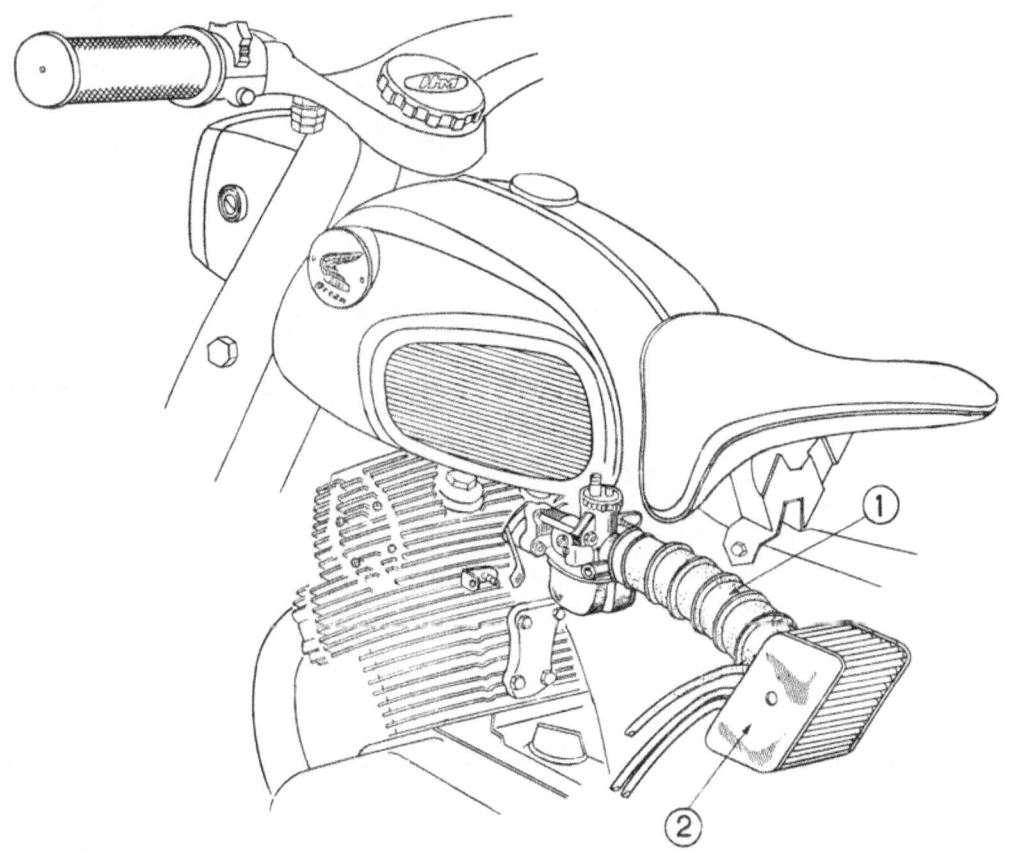

① Air cleaner connecting tube   ② Air cleaner element

Fig. 11-1. Air cleaner of Model C72, 77.

① Air cleaner connecting tube
② Air cleaner element
③ R. air cleaner support stay
④ Tool box complete
⑤ L. air cleaner support stay

Fig. 11-2. Air cleaner for CB72, 77.

B. Muffler

Construction of exhaust Muffler. Exhaust pipe conducts exhaust gas from cylinder head to muffler. Curvature of this pipe affects horse power developed exhaust gas conducted through exhaust pipe is damper inside of muffler by chocking passage and further discipate sound at the diffuser pipe to get silencing effect.

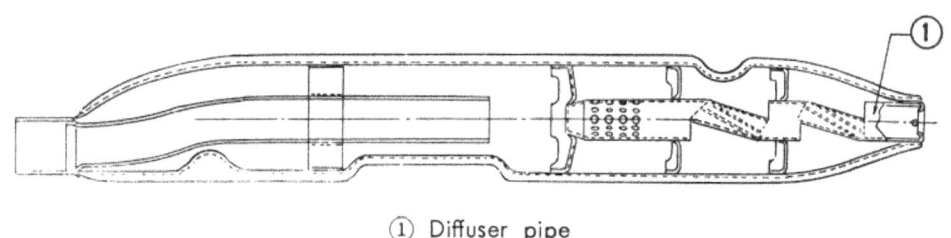

① Diffuser pipe

Fig. 11-3. Cross section of Muffler of Model C72, 77.

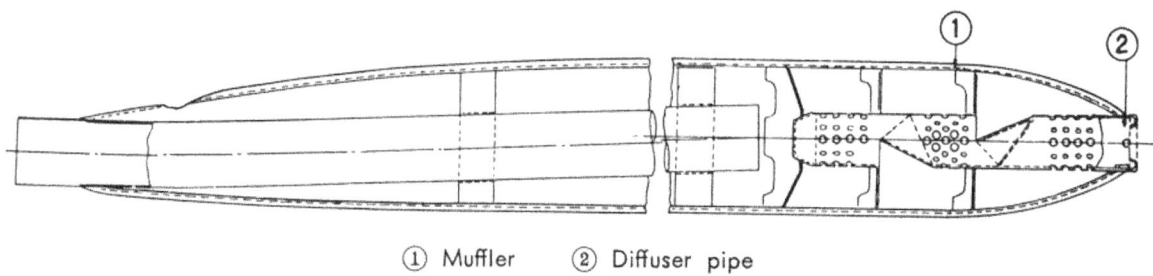

① Muffler ② Diffuser pipe

Fig. 11-4. Cross section of Muffler of Model CB72, 77

MEMO

ELECTRIC EQUIPMENT

1. Ignition system (Ignition coil, magneto, contact breaker, spark plug)
2. Electric power generator (Rotor type A.C. Generator, DC Dynamo)
3. Rectifier (Selenium rectifier)
4. Battery
5. Loading 'illumination light, winker, horn, starter)

Electric system is important part for the bicycle alike nervous system for humankind. Even a partial damage at engine ignition, light at night or horn function will affect quite often its smooth running. We adhere on JIS standard from viewpoint of manufacturing and traffic transportation vehicle law and security standard for laws & standards.

CONTENTS

1. SYSTEM

    A. Ignition Circuit 137

    B. Contact Breaker 140

    C. Condenser 143

    D. Spark Plug 144

    E. Plug Construction 145

        Wiring Diagram 150

2. CHARGING SYSTEM

    A. A.C. Generator 152

    B. Celenium Rectifier 154

    C. Battery 156

    D. Cell Starter 162

    E. Maintenance of Starting Motor 166

    F. Starter Magnetic Switch 169

3. SAFE GUARD PARTS 171

1. SYSTEM OF ELECTRIC EQUIPMENT

As ignition system, ignition coil and contact breaker are used. For electric generator, Rotor-type A.C. Generator is used, charging battery through selenium rectifier and discharging according to several loading.

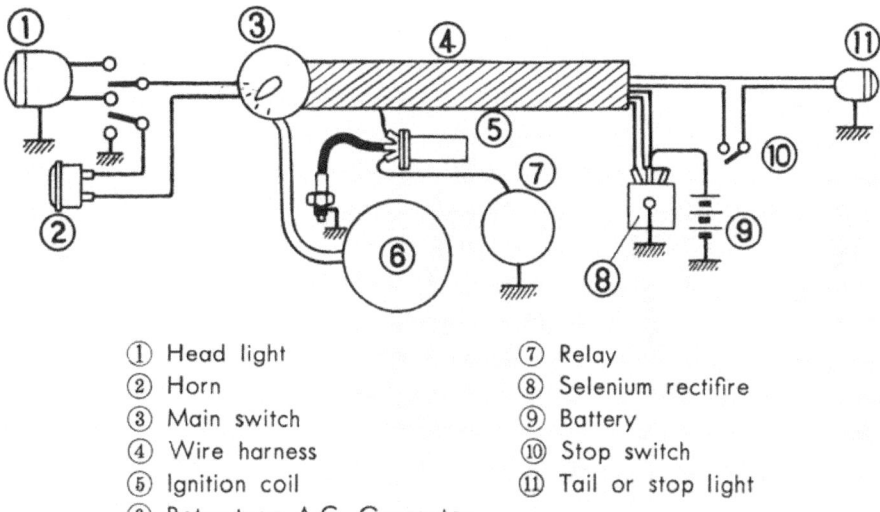

① Head light
② Horn
③ Main switch
④ Wire harness
⑤ Ignition coil
⑥ Rotor-type A.C. Generator
⑦ Relay
⑧ Selenium rectifire
⑨ Battery
⑩ Stop switch
⑪ Tail or stop light

Fig. 11-1.

A. Ignition circuit

1. Ignition system

In gasoline engine, at the favorable time of the uppermost position of compression stroke mixture gas should be burned and exploded by any means of ignition.
For both Model C. and Model CB, high tension battery ignition system is adopted (Fig. 11-2).

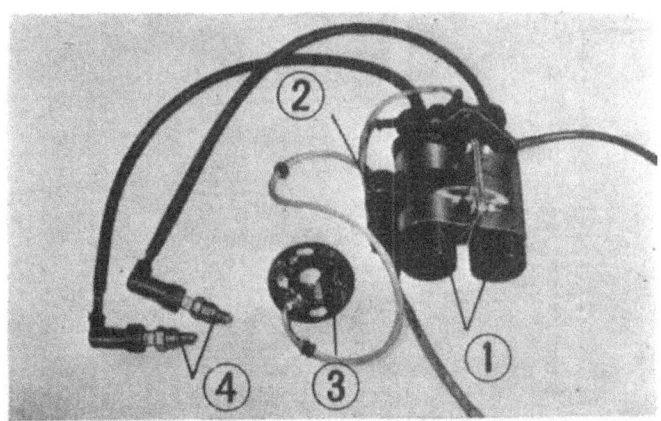

① Ignition coil
② Condenser
③ Contact breaker
④ Spark plug

Fig. 11-2. Ignition system

2. Ignition coil

Ignition coil is the same construction with that for Model C72. For Model CB72, 77-I type, there equipped with one coil each corresponding to 2 cylinders right and left, as the crank shaft angle is 180 degree. But for Model CB72, 77-II type, alike Model C72, one coil of simultaneous ignition system is equipped as the crank shaft angle is 360 degree (Fig. 11-3).

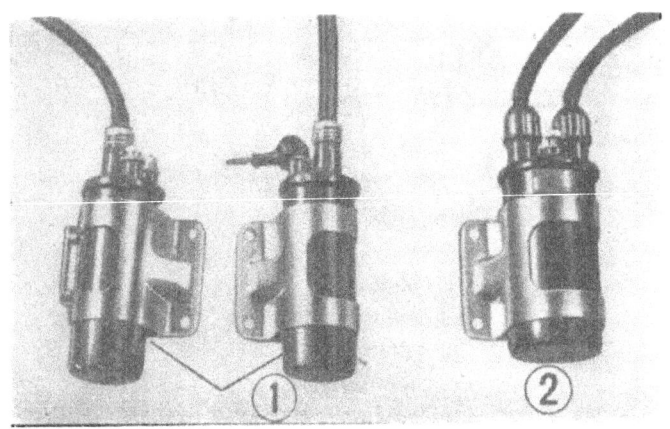

① L.R. coil for I-type
② Coil for II-type

Fig. 11- 3. Ignition coil

A. Construction of Ignition coil

Ignition coil is shown in Fig. 11-4 where fine enamel wire of 0.08 mm dia is wound over the iron core about 1 000～2 000 rounds as the secondary coil on which further enamel wire of 0.6 mm dia is wound over it about 200～300 rounds as the primary coil. And stored in the cylindrical case after insulataing process and drawing out the terminals (Fig. 11-4).

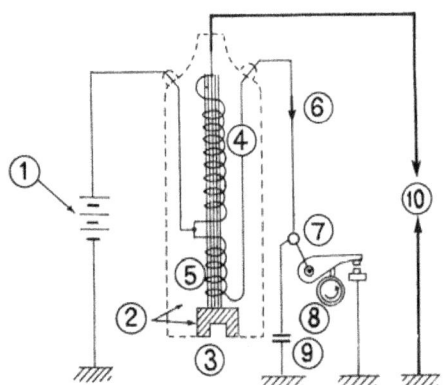

① Primary terminal
② Secondary terminal
③ Insulation
④ Iron core
⑤ Primary coil
⑥ Secondary coil

Fig. 11- 4. Cross section of Ignition coil

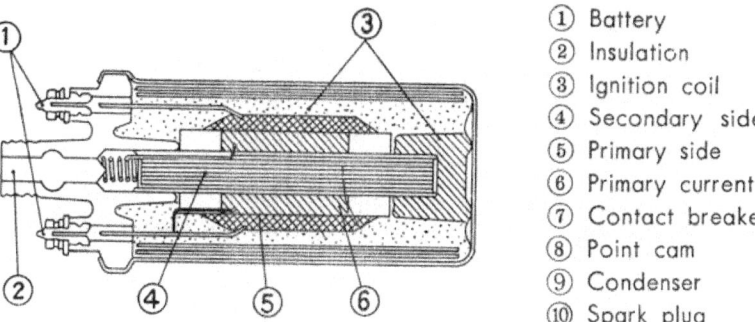

① Battery
② Insulation
③ Ignition coil
④ Secondary side
⑤ Primary side
⑥ Primary current
⑦ Contact breaker
⑧ Point cam
⑨ Condenser
⑩ Spark plug

Fig. 11-5. Function diagram of Ignition coil of Model CB72, 77.

B. <u>Function of ignition coil</u>

The principle of ignition coil is similar to that of induction coil. As shown in Fig. 11-5, rotating cam axle and crank with constant periodical relation, there generates high voltage on the secondary coil as follows.

a. When the point of the contact breaker is closed primary current flows in the directions as shown by arrow and generates magnetic flux inside the iron core.

b. When the point is opened by the cam, the magnetic flux which is generating by primary current is going to disappear suddenly.

c. Due to large variation of magnetic flux and large number of winding, there generates high voltage in the secondary coil.

d. Here generated high voltage will charge on distributed static electric volume of the secondary coil itself, then as it voltage increase, further start charging on volume of high tension cord and plug continuing increase of voltage.

e. When voltage increases up to ample amount, spark will occur at the plug gap. As soon as spark started sparking voltage drops down instantaneously. Accordingly electric load charged on the distributed static electric volume will be discharged totally. (volumetric spark). And continues discharge of energy contained in the wire by disappearing magnetic flux. (Induction spark)

f. Magnetic flux approaches down to zero instantly where voltage no more maintain spark voltage and discharging spark disappears.

g. Still energy in wire due to remaining minute magnetic flux will generate damping vibration inside secondary and primary coil, and disappear acting as resistance loss on the circuit.

h. Then returning cam angle to original state to actuate the function as stated (a) to follow the same process repeatedly (Fig. 11-5~Fig. 11-7).

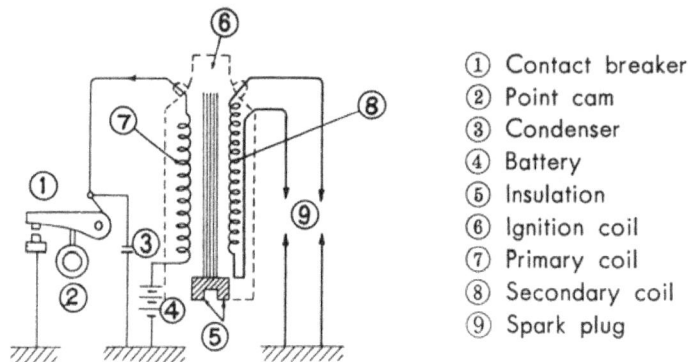

Fig. 11-6. Function of Ignition coil of Model C72, 77, CB72, 77.

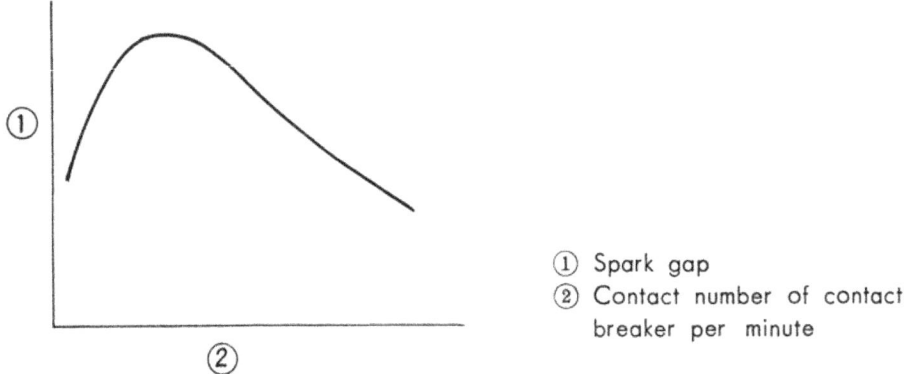

Fig. 11-7. Spark plug gap diagram.

B. Contact breaker

The contact breaker is a important part of mechanism to operate contacting and breaking the primary circuit of the ignition coil or magneto ignition coil securely. It is stored inside of the magneto for a rotary axis type magneto and fitted on the fixed stand for a combined flywheel magneto type but for separated flywheel type and battery ignition type the contact breaker is each one unit. The contact breaker is consisted of the breaker arm point on the base (movable contact point and fixed point), terminal of the primary wire, spring and oiled felt.

The breaker arm is made of bakelite impregnated with cloth or pressed thin steel attached a cam follower on its end. On its other end of each part movable contact point is fitted and insulated from base electrically.

Function of the contact breaker is required to move very lightly, so it is designed to be small size, lize, light weight and strong to make inertia small. It is necessary to put a constant spring load to avoid chattering while in short of the point. On the other hand there is other restriction of spring strength to avoid disordering of firing timing due to wear of sliding part of the cam follower.

Generally contact point pressure is designated between 700 and 900 gr. and to prevent wear of the cam follower grease should be applied on oil felt.

Required characteristics for point are as follow.

1) High unti wearing property.
2) High heat conductivity.
3) High melting point.
4) High unti oxydation.
5) Have a moderate hardness.

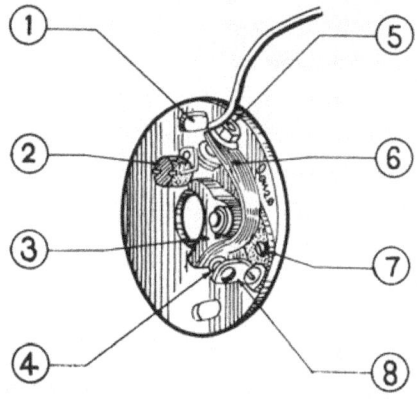

① Fixing hole of contact breaker
② Oil felt
③ Breaker arm
④ Point
⑤ Terminal
⑥ Spring
⑦ Point fixing screw
⑧ Base of contact point

Fig. 11-8.

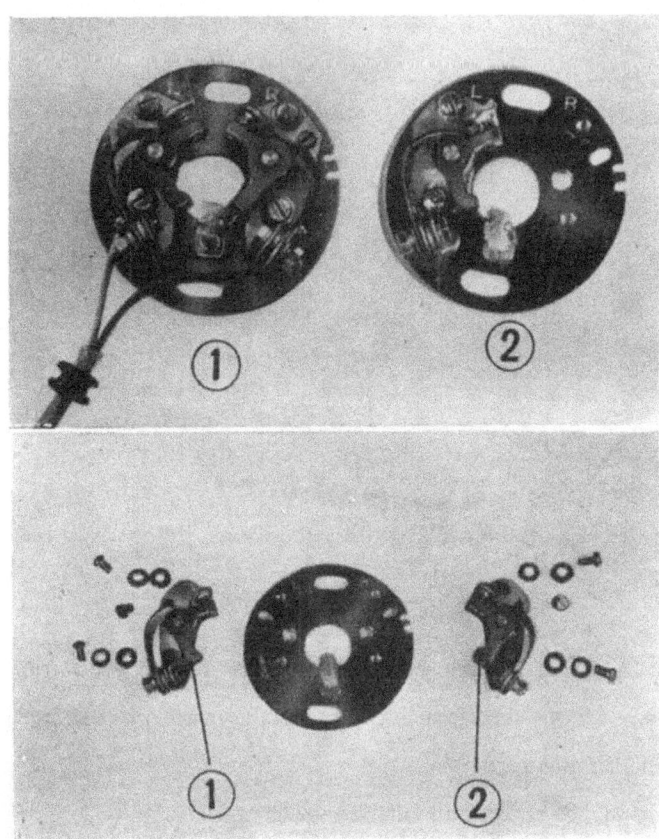

Fig. 11-9. Contact breaker assembly

① 2 points for Model CB72, 77-I type
② 1 points for Model C72, 77, for CB72, 77-II type

Fig. 11-10. Contact breaker of Model CB72, 77-I type

Generally for automotive use, 4~5 mm Tangsten is applied. Sparking is generated by magneto cam contacting and breaking of timing of crank shaft and cam shaft by the contact breaker.

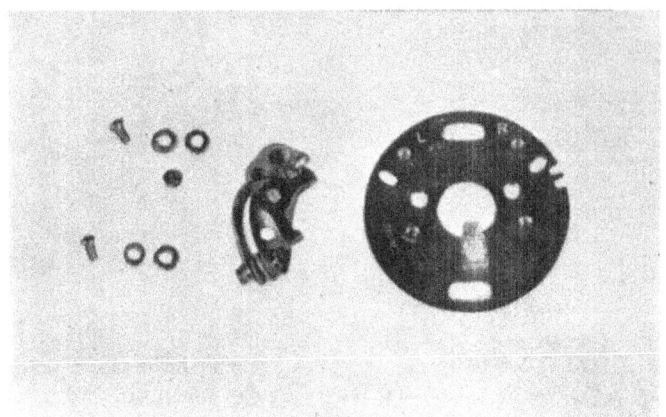

Fig. 11-11. Contact breaker of Model C72, 77, and Model CB72, 77-II type

One cam is profiled at the end of the point shaft connected with the spark advance inside of the cylinder head for Model CB72, 77-I type, and 2 sets of contact breakers are set relatively at 90 degree on the base, and designed to operate at correct timing of L and R cylinders. 2 coils, 2 points, 1 mount cam for Model CB72, 77-I type.

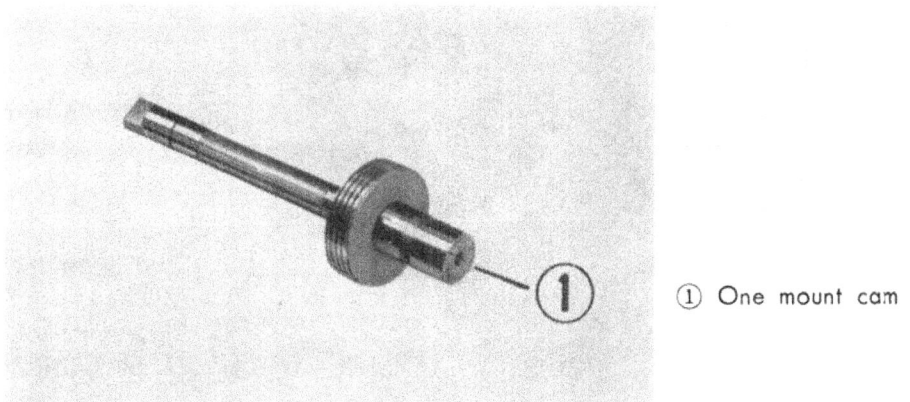

① One mount cam

Fig. 11-12. Point shaft cam profil (Model CB72, 77-I type)

For Model C72, 77 and Model CB72, 77, 2 cam are profiled on the point shaft and 1 contact breaker is fixed on the base. Here simultaneous ignition system is adopted as explained in the paragraph about the ignition coil
Model CB72, 77-II type: 1 coil, 1 point, 2 cams and simultaneous spark.

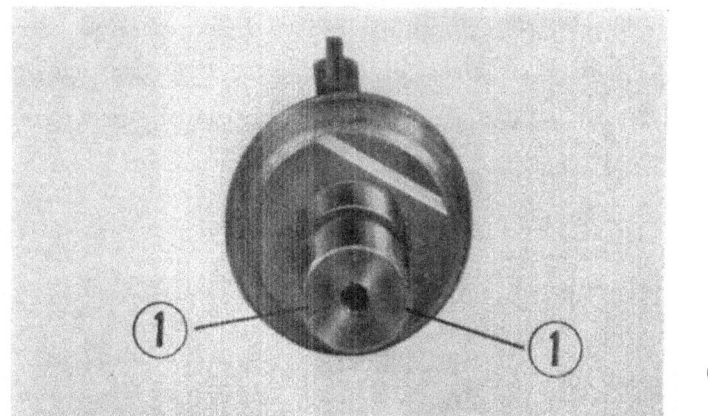

① Cam

Fig. 11-13. Point cam profil (Model CB72, 77 and Model CB72, 77-II Type

[Note]

Surface of point becomes rough with working time elapse. Especially there occurs extraordinary wear if attached oil or grease on the point surface. Further if attached oil or grease on the point surface be left alone for a long time, it solidifies and forms insulating surface to effect ignition be impossible. So special precaution is needed to prevent attaching oil.

If the surface of point becomes rough or dusty, use a fine file or sandpaper to polish and adjust, and if case is more worser, take out the contact breaker base and the breaker base and the breaker arm, polish both contact surfaces with oil stone. In this case special attention is needed to avoid one side wear. This one side wearing affects very bad influence for a new part or repaired part.

Therefore centering and parallel adjustment of both contact point is essential requirement. Also if there is found too much play within axle hole of the breaker arm it is needed to replace with new one.

On the other hand, terminals of contact breaker and insulating parts of wire have to maintain ample insulating standard, so that special precaution is required to keep clean avoiding vapour, oil, dirt to be attached. In case of adjustment of the surface of point wipe its surface with clean cloth stained with trichrene to avoid grease, oil or dirt to be attached.

C. Condenser

Function of condenser is to avoid harmful spark between points, and if taken its volume value too large spark performance becomes worse. Therefore generally it is selected adequate value between 0.1 and 0.35 microfarad.

On the other hand it is required such feature to resist high voltage as high voltage of several hundred volt acts on the condenser at the point opening instance. So it is prescribed in the JIS standard that it should resist more than one minute under such condition as A.C. 700V (50 or 60 c/s) maintaining insulation of more than 5 MΩ after heating 30 minutes at 80°C (Fig. 11-14, 11-15).

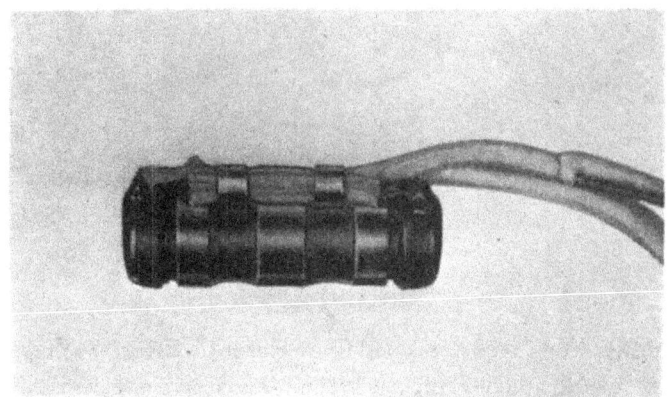

Fig. 11-14. Condenser (Model CB72, 77-I type)

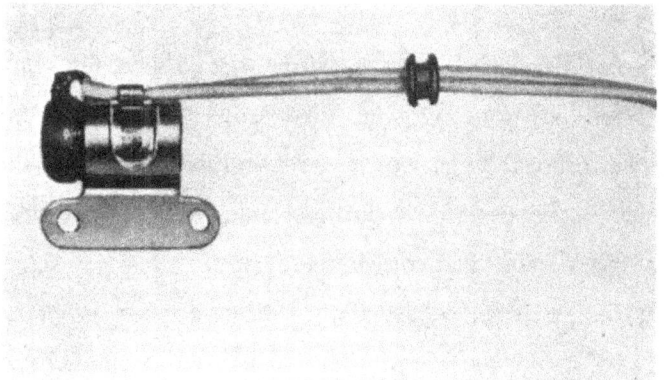

Fig. 11-15. Condenser (Model C72, 77 and Model CB72, 77-II type)

Simple test for condenser is done like the following. After checking insulating value by mega, disconnect both poles of condenser from mega while mega is running, then short both poles by wire. At this instance, if spark occurs large enough, it is decided the volume value is good standard. By use of the service tester it can be tested precisely volume value and insulating performance.

D. Spark plug

Spark plug plays the most important part within ignition system of engine, and it takes charge of starting engine, receiving high voltage generated by ignition coil or magneto to make combustion of mixture gas by high voltage spark occured spark gap within plug in the combustion chamber.

a) Conditions needed to embody for spark plug.

There are five subjects to be solved to fulfil its function perfectly, which will be explained as follows.

(A) Current: Electric current flows through the shortest way, and always tries to spark out of spark gap. At normal temperature electric insulating character of insulation is high, but at high temperature this character decreases. Therefore it is needed high insulation material which is hard to decrease its character even at high temperature.

(B) Explosion pressure

Inside the cylinder, 35~45 atmospheric pressure due to explosion always seeks path to escape. If air tightness of plug is inadequate, combustion gas of high temperature will penetrate inside it to loose its function due to overheating.

(C) Combustion head.

Temperature of combustion of mixture gas will reach up to 2000°C. It is needed to discipate this heat sooner to develop engine performance preventing over heating of plug, sparking in advance or burning electrode.

(D) Carbon in case of incomplete combustion

If get dirty on the insulating part, engine will fail its smooth running due to high voltage leaks partially and poor sparking.

(E) Lead compound

4-ethyl lead is contained in gasoline to control explosion, and lead oxidized compound is made due to combustion. If it is deposited on the plug, this compound becomes a medium having conductivity at high temperature and high voltage current will escape as explained before.

E. Construction of plug

Here is shown the plug used generally for automobile (Fig. 11-16).

a) Electrode

As material of electrode it is required to be hard to wear, low sparking voltage, high heat conductivity, high resistant to oxidation, high conductivity and easy to manufacture. At present Nickel alloy or heat resistant alloy is used (Fig. .11-17).

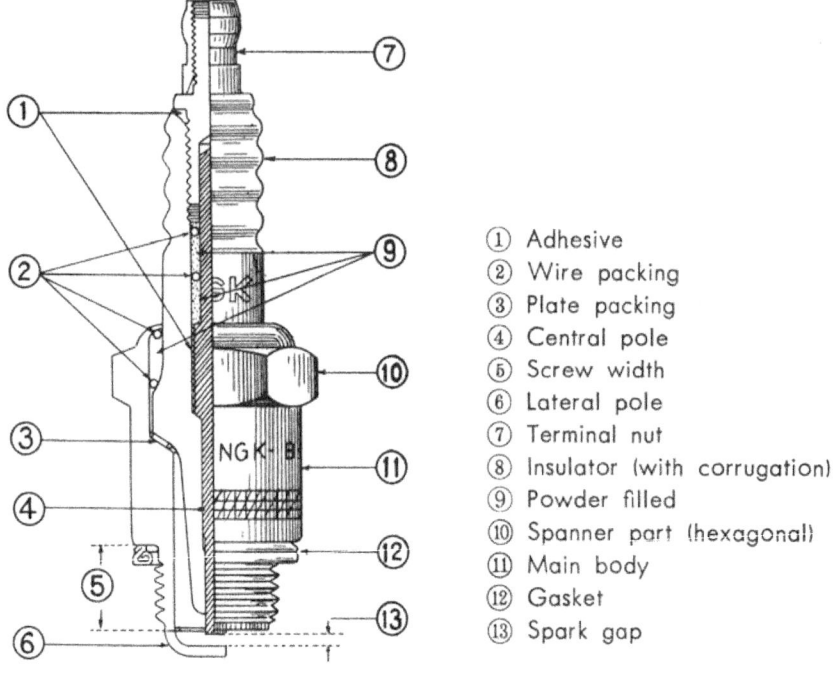

① Adhesive
② Wire packing
③ Plate packing
④ Central pole
⑤ Screw width
⑥ Lateral pole
⑦ Terminal nut
⑧ Insulator (with corrugation)
⑨ Powder filled
⑩ Spanner part (hexagonal)
⑪ Main body
⑫ Gasket
⑬ Spark gap

Fig. 11-16. Plug construction

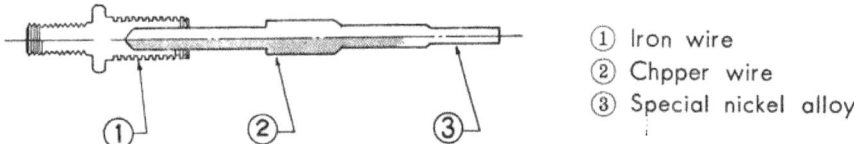

① Iron wire
② Chpper wire
③ Special nickel alloy

Fig. 11-17. Construction of electrode

b) Insulator

As insulator, special high alumina substance is used mainly. This material has a very excellent character comparing with that of famed foreign product. This superb character can be attributed to high content of alumina and a perfect material refinery process and can maintain high performance due to burning process in high temperature tunnel oven (Fig. 11-18).

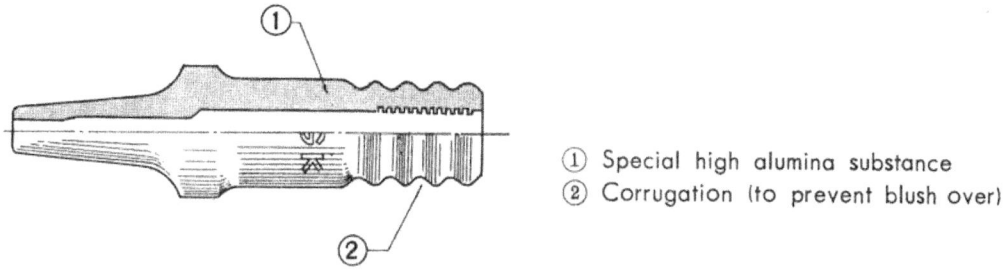

① Special high alumina substance
② Corrugation (to prevent blush over)

Fig. 11-18. Insulator

c) Concerning plug insulator (Insulator of special high alumina substance)

Characteristic of insulator and spark plug

item	Compositions		Apparent sp. gravity	Insulation resistance MΩ				Compression strength	Coefficiency of heat expansion	Coefficiency of heat conductivity	Heat shock resistance	Amount of errosion (Lead Bromide)	Amount of errosion (Lead oxide)
	Al_2O_3 %	SiO_2 %	g/cc	200°C	300°C	400°C	500C°	kg/cm²	20°C~1000°C	Cal/cm	750°C	$PbBr_2$	PbO
	90.2	7.1	3.51	∞	∞	800	80	11,800	7.8×10^{-6}	0.026~0.029	6 times	0.07	13.2

Main benefits of this insulator are as following:

(A) As insulating character is excellent, it is not rouble of misfire due to decreasing of insulating character at high speed loading condition with preventing effect of flush over by the head corrugation.

(B) Due to high heat conductivity, heat conducted to plug can be discipated quickly preventing over heat.

(C) Due to high resisting character to heat shock, there is no trouble of damage on the insulator by sudden raise and drop of heat no gas leakage due to strong construction.

To join the central electrode with insulator, and insulator with main metal body, special powder is used. This way of filling powder is prevailed method in the aircraft plug manufacturing and comparing usual cement adhesion. Air tightness is perfect for long range use accordingly central electrode can discipate heat evenly and distribute heat evenly.

Amount of wear of electrode is indistrict. Larger size of diameter of electrode is adopted to ease heat disipation and to get least wear and special alloy having heat resistant character was selected corresponding to such circumstances of high compression and high rotation. Very strict testing is done before using as even a minute crack in the material might be the cause of extraordinary wear.

d) Heat value of plug

  a) Favorable condition for plug function

Ignition part of plug is up to be dirty by carbon generated by combustion gas during engine revolution or by oil penetrated into the combustion chamber. This deposit is electric conductible itself, and makes short circuit of high voltage electricity. Accordingly weaken spark to decrease engine power misfiring and in worst case will stop engine revolution. To prevent such phenomenon surface of insulator should be heated enough to cut off carbon deposited, and this is called "self cleaning temperature". (about 450°~600°C according to engine state).

On the other hand, it burned sparking part of plug at higher temperature, sparking part will become over heated point which invites harmful knocking to burn mixture gas before hand than sparking the plug, which affect decreasing of engine power. Therefore it is requested that temperature of whole body of spark plug should be maintained less than that of premature sparking. (less than 800°C according to engine state). As a result it can be said "sparking part of plug is no good if too cooled also if too hot".

b) Escaping of heat

Heat received from combustion gas escapes as shown in the figure and sparking part maintains a certain temperature balancing heat quantity escaping and receiving.

c) Necessity of different types of plug having each different heat value.—Difference of heat quantity recieved by each plug. Heat quantity of plug received from engine depend on kinds of engine (air cooled or water cooled, 2 cycle or 4 cycle), design (compression ratio, shape of combustion chamber, plug position) and running state (speed, loading, different fuel, flat ground or climbing slope) greatly.

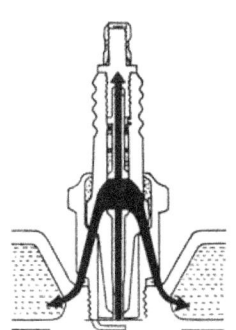

Fig. 11-19.
Way of escaping heat

Therefore it is necessary to furnish different types of plug to function satisfactorily under each different operating condition. This rate of escaping of heat is called "heat value of plug", and it is determined by its construction, form, dimension and material. It is called "cold type" (for high temperature use) which disipates heat easily and is hard to be over heated, and on the contrary such types as hard to disipate heat and easy to be heated is called "Hot type" (low temperature use).

In Fig. 11-20, difference between types functionally are shown.

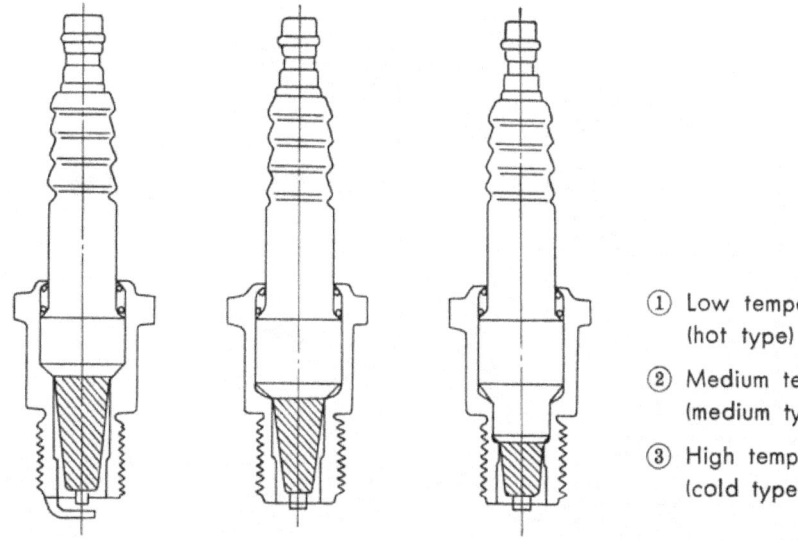

Fig. 11-20. Different plug for heat condition

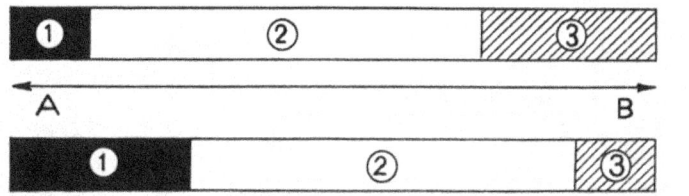

① Dirty
② Smooth running
③ Ignition too early
A; Low power
B; High power

Fig. 11-21. Hot type plug (for low temperature use)

MEMO

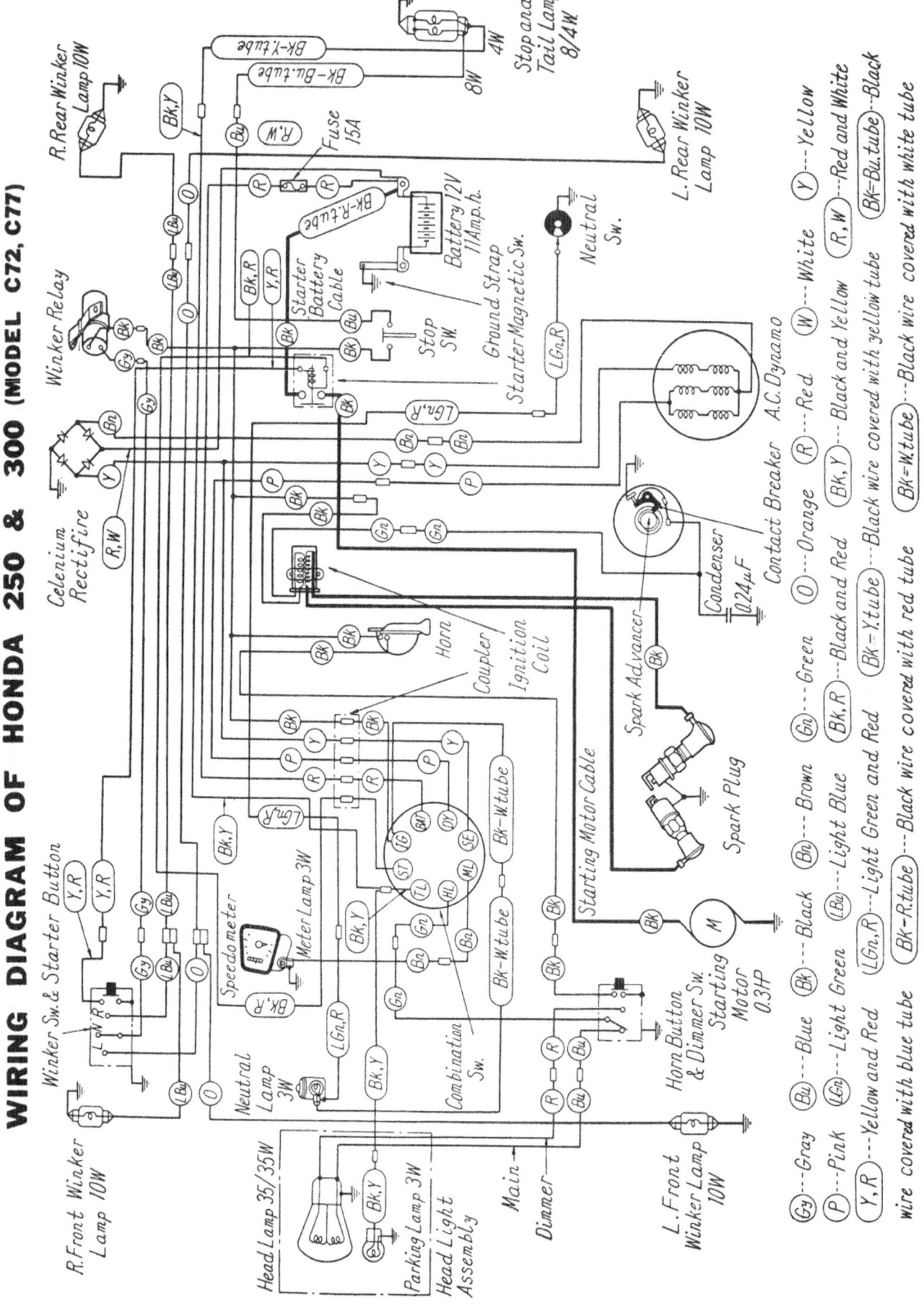

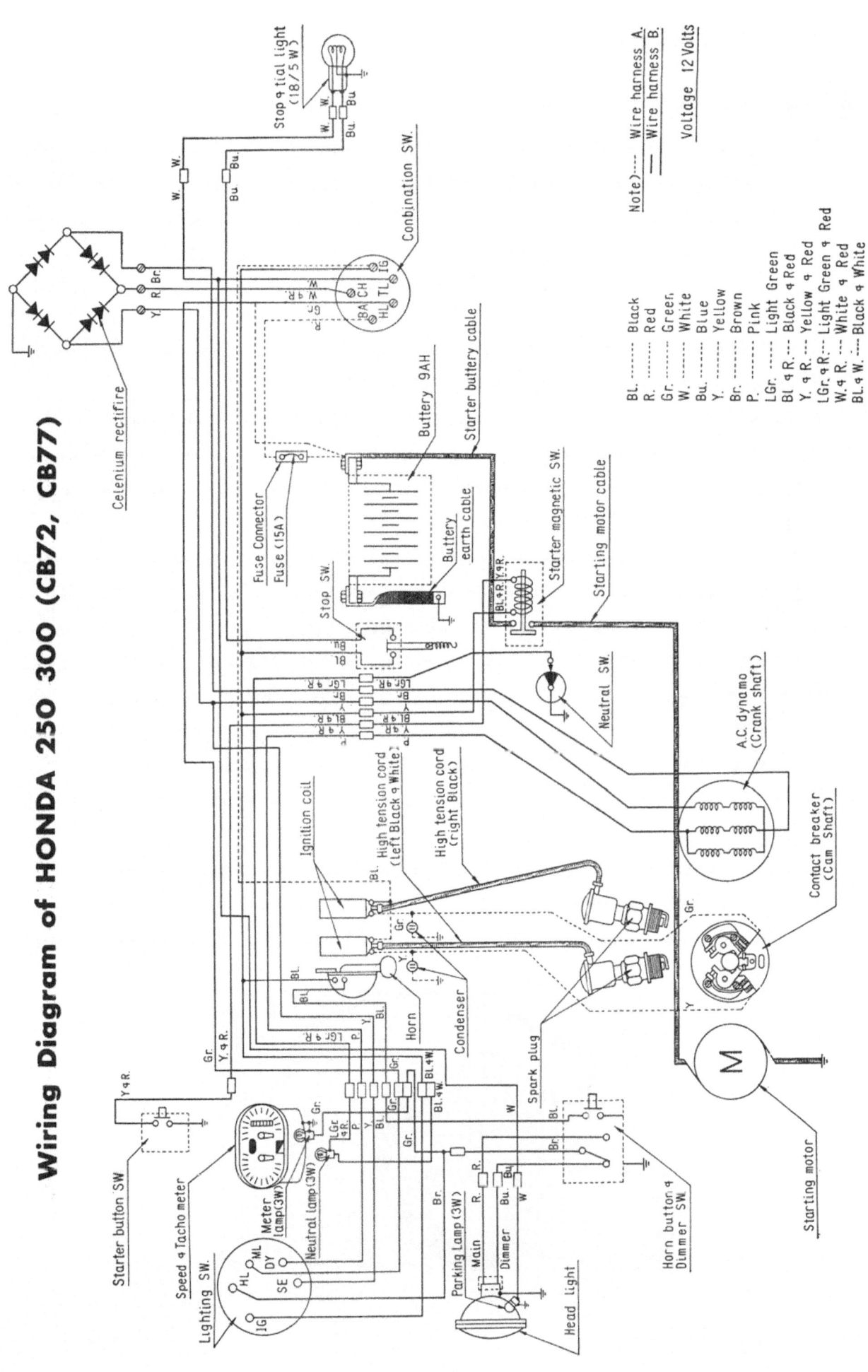

2. CHARGING SYSTEM

A. Rotor-type A.C. Generator

The principle of generation of electricity by Rotor-type A.C. Generator is same as that of the flywheel magnets. Magnetic flux in the iron core of coil turn its direction as much times as number of magnetic pole for each a turn of the magnetic iron. For each a turn of the magnetic iron, as magnetic flux in the iron core changes with

$$\frac{\text{magnetic pole number}}{2}$$

cycles (3 cycles per one turn for 6 poles Generator), so there generates A.C. voltage in the generating coil due to this variation of magnetic flux.

The more magnetic force of magnetic iron, and the earlier rate of change of magnetic flux in the core (the more quick the rotation of magnetic iron, and the more number of magnetic poles) and also the more number of winding of coil, the large A.C. voltage is generated (Fig. 11-22, 11-24).

All these conditions couldn't be satisfied from viewpoint of manufacturing, and among magnetic force of magnetic iron, number of magnetic poles and number of winding of coil there is such inter relation as to increase one sacrificing other. Due to defects of Rotor-type A.C. Generator (Flywheel, generating coil of Generator), which works with wrong voltage variation and not equipped with a voltage regulator, there occur too much raise or drop of voltage if take the loading at random not using regular loading. But recently these defects have been overcome by magnets manufacturers' effort.

On the other hand for magnetic weakening of magnetic iron preventive measures have been taken in the course of design. (Fig. 11-23)

A point of excellence of Rotor-type A.C. Generator due to it simple and strong construction is almost no trouble and lack of wear parts. Special feature of using Rotor-type A.C. Generator combined with ignition coil is to make it possible emergency starting

Fig. 11-22. Rotor-type A. C. Generator

which is impossible to be followed by Rotor-type A.C. Generator. Frequently there occurs perfect discharging carelessly from capacity Battery mounted on motor cycle, due to its small capacity.

For the battery ignition system, it is impossible to spark unless replacing battery or recharging, but for the Rotor-type A.C. Generator system it is still possible to spark by kicking even after perfect discharging of battery due to its feature of steep and high induction voltage of Rotor-type A.C. Generator under light load where generated voltage be conducted to ignition coil in D.C. or A.C. as it is through celenium rectifier.

Therefore it enables emergency starting by switching of adequate circuit connection.

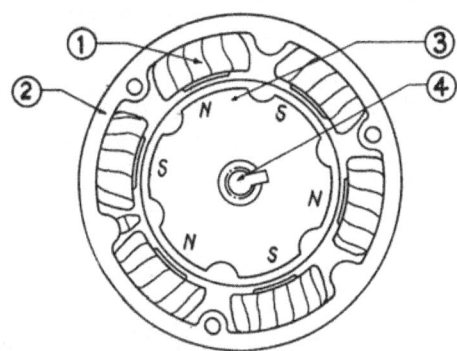

① Coil
② Fixed core (iron core and coil)
③ Rotor (magnetic iron)
④ Crank shaft

Fig. 11-23. Construction of Rotor-type A.C. Generator

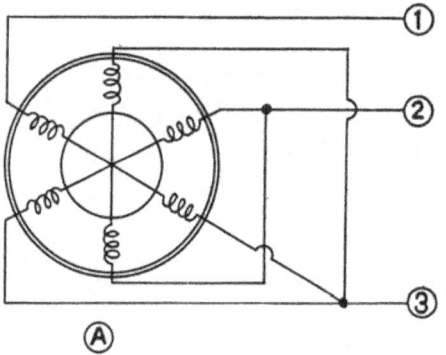

A; Generator
① Yellow (usual use)
② White (day and night)
③ Brown (common use)

Fig. 11-24. Circuit diagram of Rotor-type A.C. Generator

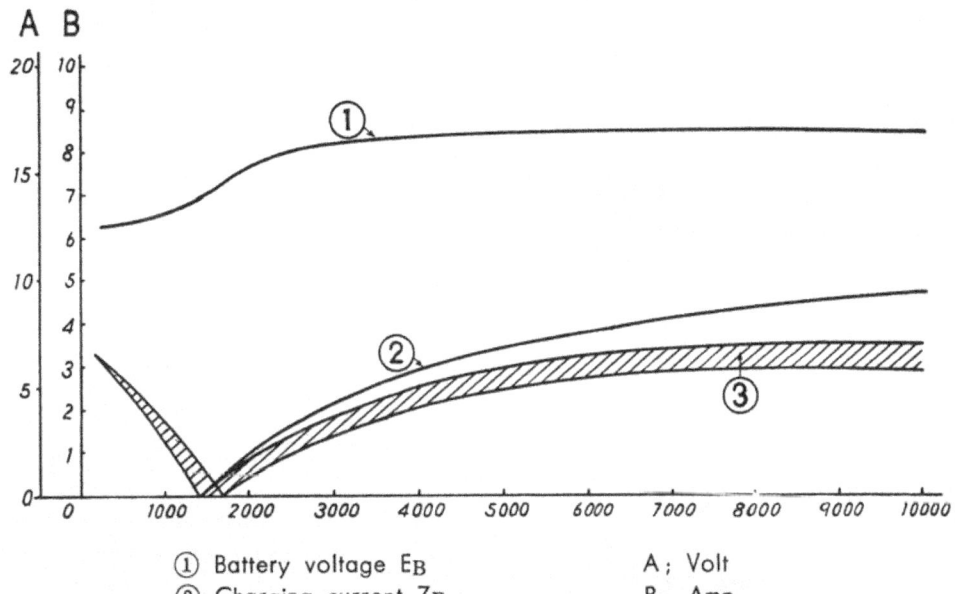

① Battery voltage E_B
② Charging current Z_B

A; Volt
B; Amp

Fig. 11-25.-(a) Characteristics of Rotor-type A.C. Generator (daytime)

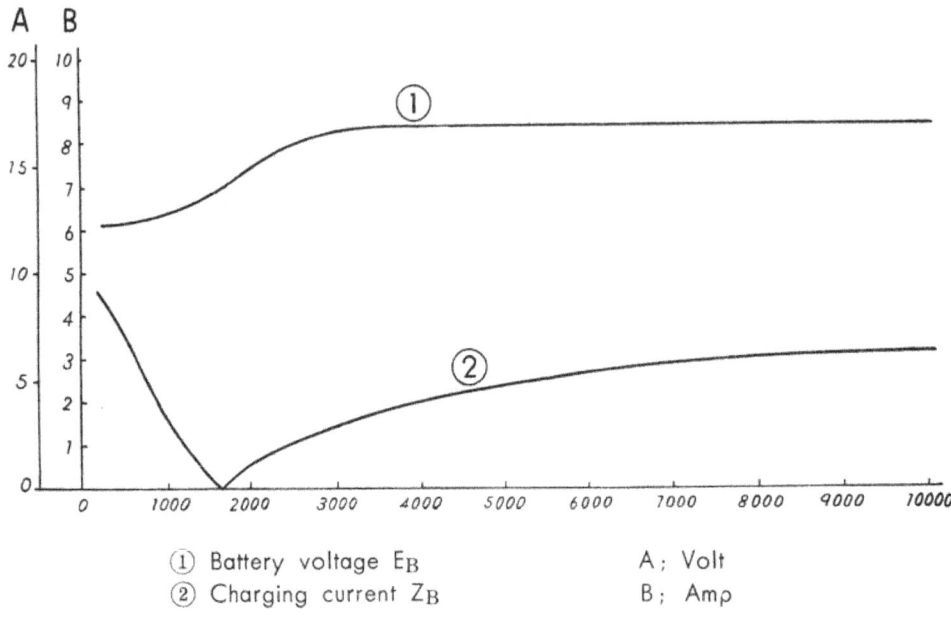

① Battery voltage E_B A; Volt
② Charging current Z_B B; Amp

Fig. 11-25.-(b) Characteristics of Rotor-type A.C. Generator (during night)

B. Celenium rectifier

The celenium rectifier is used for rectifying the D.C. current from the A.C. current, always combined with Rotor-type A.C. Generator or AC generating coil.

There are several kinds of construction, material and form for this rectifier, but the principle is same utilizing its special character of easy flow of current to one direction and closing to other. Types of rectifier generally used are celenium rectifier, copper oxide rectifier, and germanium rectifier. Rectifying unit to rectify by the selenium rectifier is shown is Fig. 11-26(a), and is composited by rectifying plates combined with end plates

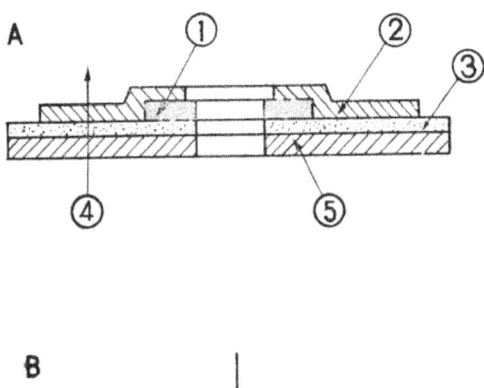

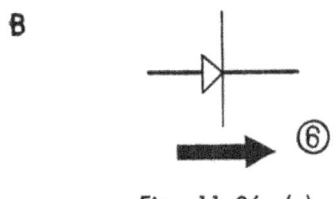

Fig. 11-26.-(a)

(A) Rectifying plate
①
② Electric pole
③ Selenium
④ Positive direction
⑤ Bare plate (nickel plated steel or aluminum)
(B) A sign of rectifier or rectifying plate
⑥ Direction of current

and spacers of required number in series or parallel and further according to rectifying system it is set in comb-like arrangement on different rectifying circuit style.

Rectifying plate is shown in Fig. (A), where on the base steel sheet or alminium plate of nickel plated circular or rectangular form, refined selenium mixed with a adequate amount of impurity is spattered in vacuum and further ready fusable alloy of Cd, Bi or Sn is poured on its surface to make electric pole after perfect heat treatment to make it active metal selenium.

Then it becomes possible to get such phenomenon as current is easy to flow to positive direction and almost shut to flow to another direction if put current to the reverse direction to that shown by arrow. This is called rectifying action of selenium rectifying plate. This characteristics caused by unsymmetric conductivity due to the layer of barrier on the contacting surface between pole and metal selenium of semi conductivity. As moisture is very harmful effect on the selenium rectifying plate, anti-moisture processing is done by moisture resistant paint to prevent corrosion.

The selenium rectifying unit which is common for Model C72, 77 and Model CB72, 77 is connected in bridge and number of selenium rectifying plate becomes much and the ignition coil works for both cycles of positive and negative loading. Durability of the selenium rectifier depends on temperature largely, and it is prohibitted to raise more than 30°C. So is requested not to flow over current for a longtime.

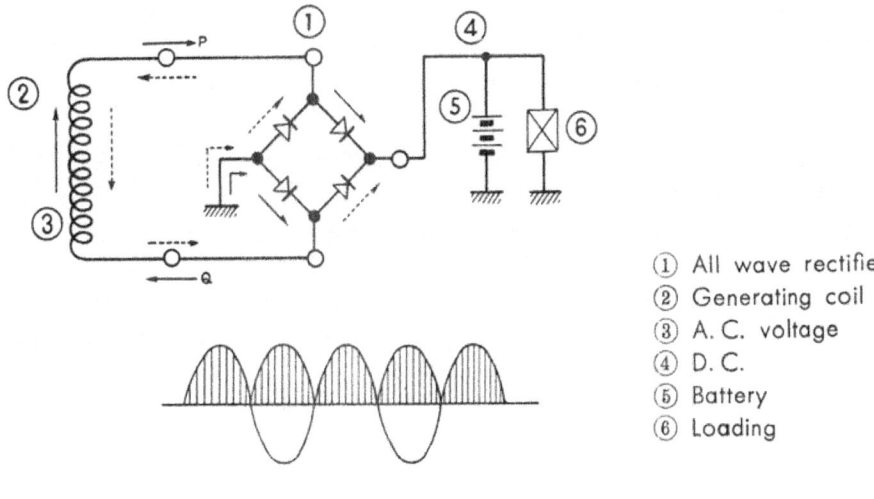

① All wave rectifier
② Generating coil
③ A. C. voltage
④ D. C.
⑤ Battery
⑥ Loading

Fig. 11-26.-(b)

On the other hand, there is so-called resisting reverse voltage which more voltage is put to reverse direction there occurs puncture (Here punctured part turns to be insulating substance at once and this damage self-restores its function reducing effective rectifing area. The more number of puncture, the more rectifying efficiency will be decreased to be overheated). Therefore it is necessary to raise total resisting reverse voltage by putting required number of plates in series corresponding to A.C. voltage generated by the generator coil.

In Fig. 11-26(b), put A.C. voltage between terminals P.Q. of the generating coil as (A) : (B) : (C) = 1 : 2 : 1, it is evident (C) is most suitable for high A.C. valtage rectifier as the reverse voltage per one rectifying plate is smallest. Generally speaking is selenium rectifying system for use of automotive A.C. generating coil (C) > (B) > (A) is the order to select corresponding to voltage.

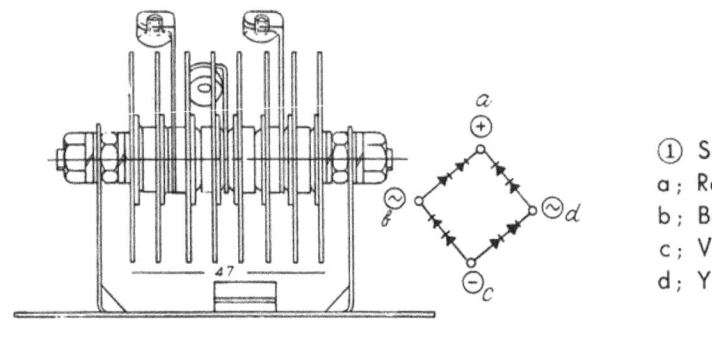

① Selenium rectifier ass'y
a ; Red terminal
b ; Brown terminal
c ; Volt
d ; Yellow terminal

Fig. 11-26.-(c)

Remarks :

Special precaution is necessary in using selenium rectifier not to run engine under such condition as no loading state (for instance unloading state of battery during daytime or taking out state yellow of fuse), as high voltage generated by generating coil under no load or light load condition acts to the reverse direction. This leads to puncture trouble and will damage the selenium rectifier if continued a long time.

On the other hand, there occurs ageing change in the selenium rectifier for a long term use increasing internal resistance in the rectifier plate to decrease output voltage and to increase temperature.

The largest cause of ageing change is temperature raise and at more than 70°C in the rectifier this change occurs rapidly, therefore it is required to select cool position to equip it.

There is such tendency as to increase current to reverse direction if selenium rectifier has not been used for a long time. In such case, before using raise voltage slowly during one hour from lower voltage (about half of standard) to restore its function.

C. Battery

All the battery for automotive use are lead storage battery and its construction is as shown in the figure i.e. anode plate group and cathode plate group (one plate more than anode group) are put together in turn inserting separator between anode & cathode plates, and these combined plates are stored in the cell (ebonite or stirol made) dipped with electrolysis solution. One unit as shown in the figure is called an unit cell and generates about 2.1 Volt (in case of perfect charge, this will be up to 2.5 V during charging).

For Model C72, 77 6 V is used and for Model CB72, 77 12 V is used, connecting each cell of each 3 piece or 6 piece by connecting rod in series.

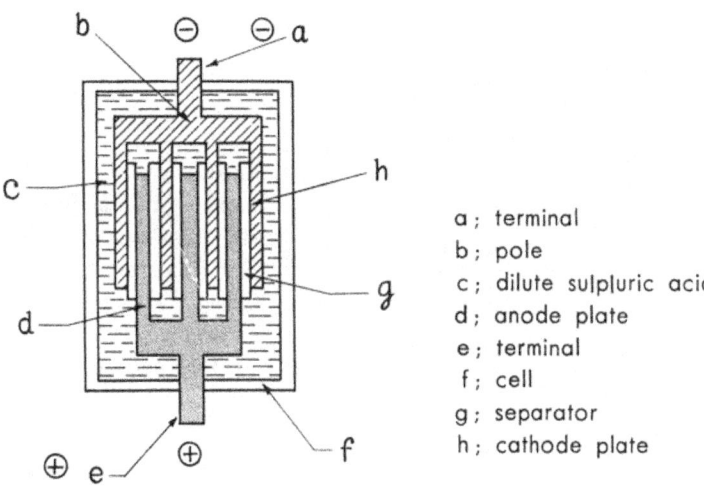

a ; terminal
b ; pole
c ; dilute sulpluric acid
d ; anode plate
e ; terminal
f ; cell
g ; separator
h ; cathode plate

Fig. 11-27. Storage battery

The pole plate is made of lead antimony lattice painted with powder of lead oxide in paste state and dried. For anodic plate, hard lead oxide in dark brown color is filled up and for cathode plate gray porous sponge like lead is filled.

There contains expanding substance to prevent contracting solidification while in use as for separator thin cypress sheet (recently rubber sheet with fine holes or sythetic plates are used) is used, and glass mat is inserted between anodic plate and separator to prevent oxidation of separator and dropping substance of anodic action.

There occurs discharge when connected load between both terminals of battery, and gradually substance of both pole plate changes to lead sulphate, accordingly, specific gravity of dilute sulphuric acid will decrease to drop terminal voltage. This rate of decrease of specific gravity is proportional to amount of discharge approximately as shown in Fig (a). So it will be determined amount of discharge or remaining amount by checking variation of specific gravity if known the initial specific gravity (sg. at complete charge 1.260 and sg. at complete discharge 1.10). Specific gravity of dilute sulphuric acid varies with change of temperature. If also depend on the kind of battery but generally about 1,260 is selected with converting standard temperature 20°C.

If put current on the discharged battery in the direction reversal to discharging, lead sulphate generated on both plates restore their original state, i.e. become lead oxide and sponge lead again, and specific gravity of dilute sulphuric acid increase gradually and increase terminal voltage as charging progress.

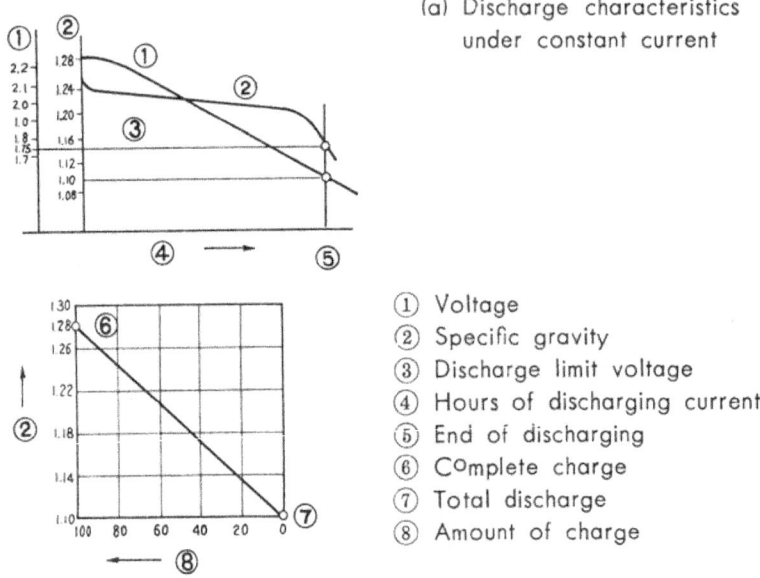

(a) Discharge characteristics under constant current

① Voltage
② Specific gravity
③ Discharge limit voltage
④ Hours of discharging current
⑤ End of discharging
⑥ Complete charge
⑦ Total discharge
⑧ Amount of charge

Fig. 11-28. Battery

a) Volume and rate of discharge (rate of charging)

Volume of battery is defined as amount of volume dischargeable down to discharge end voltage at terminals regulated by JIS from complete charged battery discharging under constant current. (mean value 1.575 V per each unit cell) To express its value Ampere hour (Ah) (discharging current times discharging hours) is used.

Volume of battery depends on temperature of discharging current and specific gravity. As conditions of volumes test regulated by JIS for use of battery for motor cycle, specific gravity of electrolysis solution should be $1,260 \pm 0,005$ (converted to 20°C), current 10 hours rate, and temperature of solution $25 \pm 2°C$. Concerning rate of discharge, given here the battery completely charged, discharge down to the end discharge voltage with X ampere within T hours, volume of this battery is expressed by XT ampere-hours (Ah), and X ampere is called the current of rate of discharge of T hours.

Therefore battery of 10 hours rate volume 11 Ah means such capacity as to discharge 10 hours down to the end discharge volt and current of 10 hours rate of discharge is 11A. Similarly for charging current, it is expressed 10 hours rate of charging. To express amount of charging or discharging current, duration of time in hours down to the end discharging volt is used.

b) Initial charging

Battery can be stored after assembly for a fairy long time, if not electrolysis solution be poured in and seal tightly a pouring orifice. Therefore when battery not charged yet is to be used initial charging is necessary. This is done after pouring electrolysis solution charging with regular initial charging current for about 70 hrs. continuously to attain both pole plates a perfect charging state for the first time.

It is required the initial charging should be done perfectly, otherwise this battery will not display its volume 100% for future use and its life be shorten seriously.

Precaution necessary before starting for use;

Inspection should be done before use of Battery finished initial charging as follow:

(1) Inspect if there is something unusual or not, as damage, happens sometimes during transportation. Especially due to damage on the case there happens leakage of solution.

(2) Peep inside through pouring port after taking cap, or check the level of solution to be on regular height. If its level is lower, check damage if any on the case. If no damage, supplement dilute sulphuric acid of same specific gravity with other. cell.

(3) If time elapsed more than two weeks after the initial charging, it is necessary to supplement charge to supply amount of self discharged electricity while let alone. During this supplement charging, it is desirable to check level of solution to adjust regular height and further measure and keep record of voltage, specific gravity and temperature for each cell for future reference.

Fig. 11-29. Supplement charging of Battery

Precautions while in use;

1) Inspect battery periodically, once a week for automotive use. At least twice a month or after each 1 000~2 000 km running.

2) Special attention should be paid on the level of solution and if short supply distilled water or drinking water (no content of metal as Ferrous). If the case of battery is transparent there is shown level of solution, but generally the height of solution should be adjusted about 13 mm over the separator. If the pole plate be exposed in the air due to drop of level, there occurs oxidation on the plate making white sulphuric lead which decrease volume of battery, and effect the performance of exposed plate to be serious cause of inner shorting. So many troubles are experienced due to this cause, therefore it wouldn't be exaggeration to say that is the most part of causes to shorten it life.

3) Keep always in charged state. If used for a long time in insufficient charged state trouble called sulphation will be accelerated and at last it invites such difficulty as to make it hard to restore original substance by usual charging. Such pole plate warps easy to short. On the other hand, if used with thin solution due to over discharging separator gets damage. Therefore it is requested to supplement change before the discharge limit. (Fig. 11-29~11-31).

Fig. 11-30. Sign of level of solution

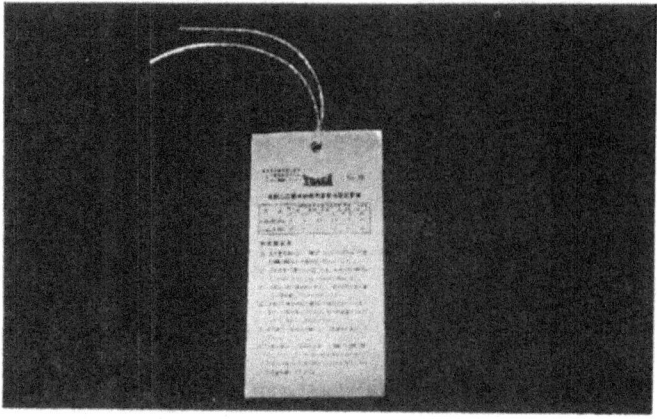

Fig. 11-31. Precaution for use

For the battery, MBJ4-12 type (Voltage 12 V, volume 10 hours rate 10 Ah) is applied. Duration of battery is expressed by hours from the complete charging state to the complete discharged state using electricity for each separate loading while in stationary state. Therefore if the loading overlapped duration will be shorten so much. This relation could be presumed from the following table.

Kinds of loading on battery	Standard	Mean consumption of current	duration of battery (approximate)
Head light	35/35 W	3 A	2 hrs
Cell motor	0.4 kW	10 ~ 50 A	Listed on other part
Magnetic starter switch	—	3.5 A	"
Neutral lamp	3 W	0.25 A	40 hrs
Winker lamp	10 W × 2	1 A	10 hrs
Tail light	4 W	0.35 A	30 hrs
Stop light	8 W	0.7 A	
Speed meter lamp	3 W	0.25 A	40 hrs
Ignition	Stop —	* 3.5 A	1.6 hrs
	Running —	0.8 ~ 1.2 A	—
Horn	100 P	1.5 A	6 hrs

*In case of Point clased and switch on

For instances, if the head light 35 W is on, consumption is 3 A only and duration will be about 2 hrs. but if the tail lamp (0.35A) and ignition (3.5A) were used simultaneously total consumption will be 6.85A. From the figure above shown duration becomes 35~40 minutes.

While in running, charging is done corresponding to engine revolution, so that difference between charging and discharging current will behave charging or discharging.

    Charging current > discharging current

        →charge battery

    Charging current < discharging current

        →discharge battery

Especially as large current flows while in use of cell motor, it is required to control less than 5 seconds for one action, after that takes rest 10~15 sec to repeat next action.

There occurs rapid drop of voltage if large current taken out from the battery but it restores the original voltage if taken a rest.

Therefore continuous pushing on the Cell Button causes voltage drop preventing restoration to the effect of early exhaustion.

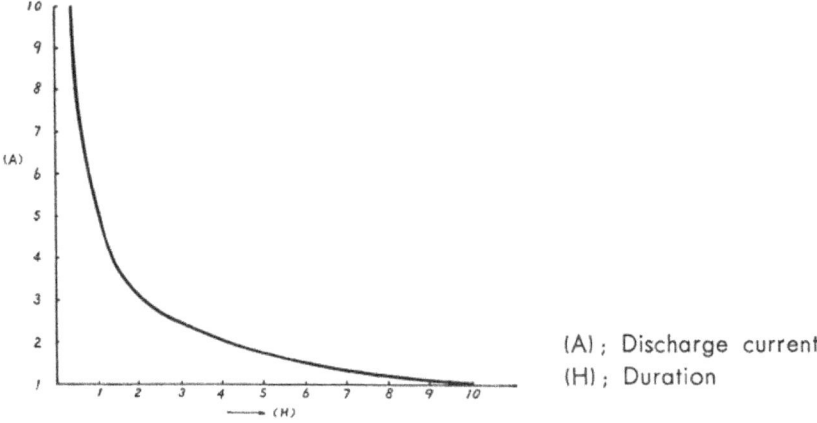

(A); Discharge current
(H); Duration

Fig. 11-32. Relation between discharge current and duration for MBJ 4-12 type (12 V, 10 AH) battery.

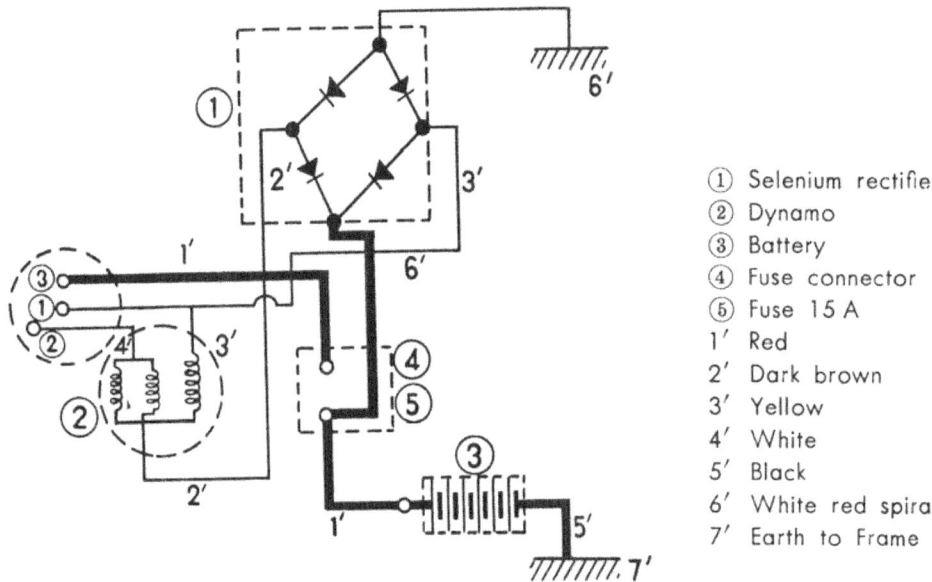

① Selenium rectifier
② Dynamo
③ Battery
④ Fuse connector
⑤ Fuse 15 A
1' Red
2' Dark brown
3' Yellow
4' White
5' Black
6' White red spiral
7' Earth to Frame

Fig. 11-33. Charging current circuit diagram.

D. Cell Starter

a) Starting Circuit

The starter switch of push button style is equipped on the right side of the handle. Pushing it, the starter magnetic switch is operated to feed current of about 100A to the starting motor from the battery for Model C 72, 77, and about 60A for Model CB 72, 77 to rotate the starting motor.

The starting motor is equipped in front of the crank case and the crank shaft is rotated by starting chain through the overrunning clutch from the dynamo side.

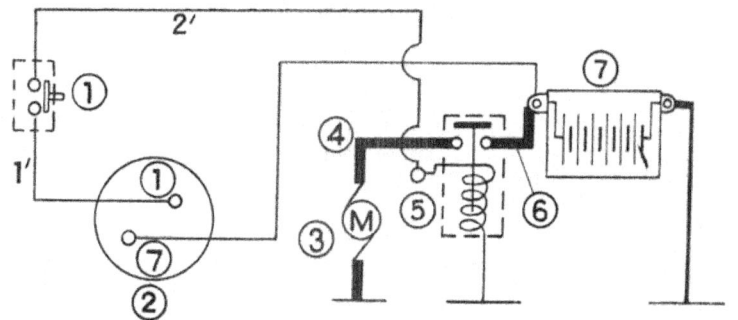

Fig. 11-34. Wiring of Cell starter

① Starter switch
② Combination switch
③ Starting motor
④ Starting motor cable
⑤ Starter magnetic switch
⑥ Starter battery cable
⑦ Battery
1′ Black red spiral
2′ Yellow red spiral

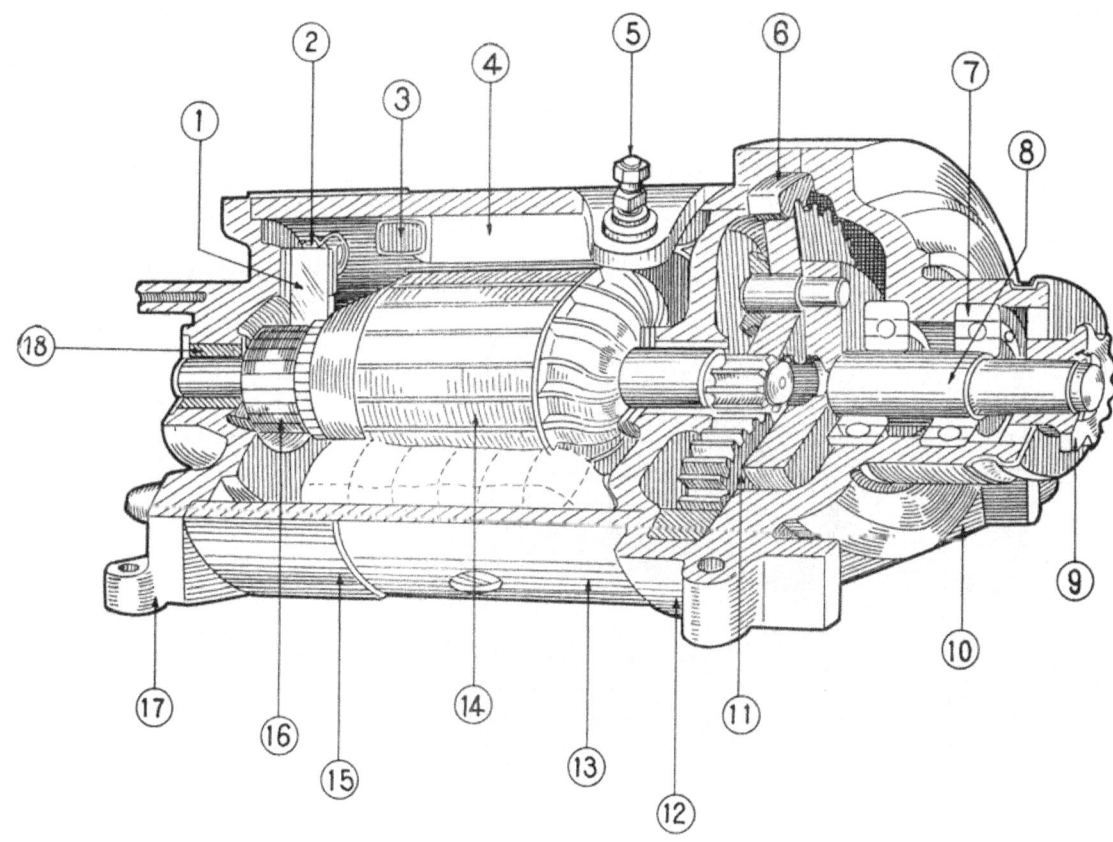

Fig. 11-35. Starter motor

① Brush
② Brush spring
③ Field coil
④ Pole core
⑤ Terminal
⑥ Internal gear
⑦ Ball bearing
⑧ Sprocket shaft
⑨ Sprocket
⑩ Gear housing
⑪ Planetary gear
⑫ Center bearing holder
⑬ York
⑭ Armature
⑮ Cover band
⑯ Comutator
⑰ Comutator end frame
⑱ Bearing bush

b) Reduction of starter

To get required torque and revolution to rotate the crank shaft by reducing revolution of the motor mechanical reduction is necessary. To complete this in high weight the primary reduction is done by planetary gear and further the secondary reduction by starting chain.

    Primary reduction ratio   5,78 : 1 (planetary gear)
    Secondary ,,   ,,   2,77 : 1 (chain)
    Total reduction ratio   1691 : 1

As the starting motor does not run constantly there seldom occurs wear but to prevent moisture its construction is closed type.

Therefore after each 5,000~10,000 km run the following points should be checked with care.

① Check wearing on carbon brush and commutator.
② Eliminate carbon powder (blow off by compressed air).
③ Supply grease in the gear case.

If required by any reason to take out the starting chair, do not disassemble the starting sprocket from the motor.

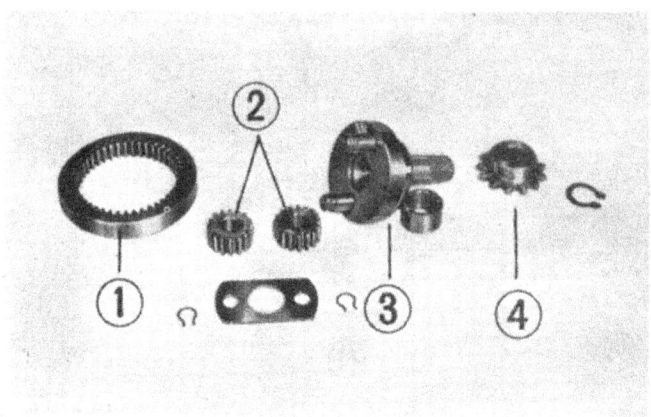

① Internal gear
② Planet gear
③ Sprocket shaft
④ Sprocket

Fig. 11-36.

Fig. 11-37. Cell-motor attached on Engine

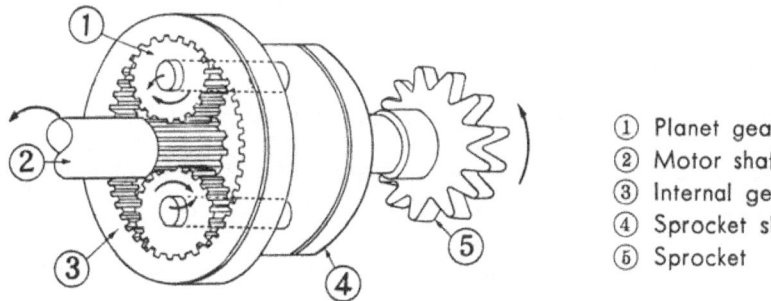

① Planet gear
② Motor shaft
③ Internal gear
④ Sprocket shaft
⑤ Sprocket

Fig. 11-38. Reduction mechanism

By any chance if the starting sprocket were taken out it is necessary to disassemble even the planetary gear and the starting sprocket should be combined before reassemble the starting motor.

If the sprocket were set in, without disassemblying the starting motor by mistake there happens rotation impossible due to hitting against the case by the planetary gear. (Fig. 11-36~11-38)

c) Dismounting the Starting Motor

   a. Take off the starting motor cable from terminal.

   b. Loosen each two screws of 6 mm tightening the starting sprocket cover and take off the cover.

   c. Loosen two screws of 5 mm on the starting motor side cover and take off the side cover.

   d. While loosening 4 bolts of 6 mm fitted on the crank case and taking out the starting motor from the engine case, it will be seperated from engine by removing the stanting sprocket from the chair. (Fig. 11-39)

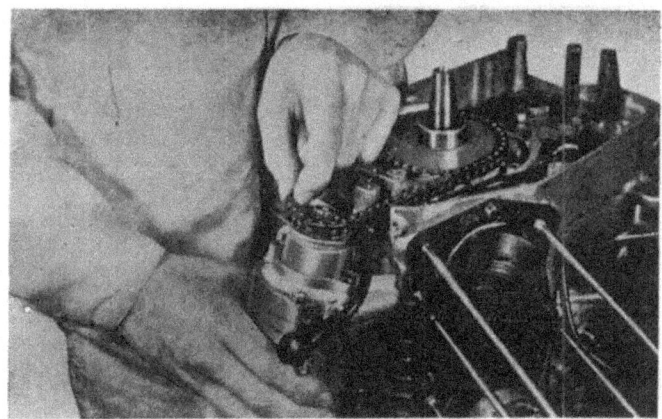

Fig. 11-39.

E. Maintenance of the Starting Motor.

1. Removal of the carbon brush.

   a. Take off the cover band complete of the commutator.

   b. Loose 2 bolts fitted on the commutator end frame and take it out.

   c. By taking out the carbon brush pressing spring, take out the carbon brush loosening the connecting screw of the field coil and carbon brush.

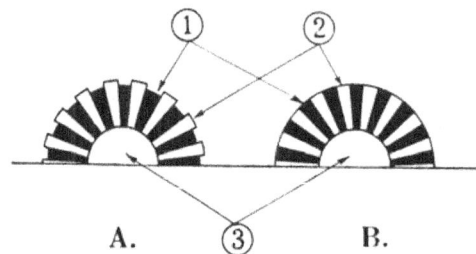

① Mica piece
② Commutator (Cu)
③ Motor shaft

Fig. 11-40. Cross section of commutator

2. Commutator

   The commutator is as shown in Fig. (A) while in use copper pant get wear to turn like (B).

   In such cases its is requested to adjusts to be (A).

   It is advisable to rely on specialist shops as this adlustment requires high techniques (under cutting of mica) (Fig. 11-40)

① A.C. Generator rotor
② Starting clutch-outer
③ 10.2×11.5 roller

Fig. 11-41. Generator srotor and tarting clutch

F. Over running clutch

This transmit rotation from the starting motor to the crank shaft, but reversaly from the crank shaft can not rotate the starting motor.

This construction is quite same with Model C72. (Fig. 11-41)

1. If turns the starting motor
   a. When the starting chain is pulled along the direction of arrow as shown in the picture.
   b. By rotating the sprocket, the clutch outer is turned when the roller is joined with the starting sprocket and the clutch outer moving to the narrower side. Accordingly the dynamo rotor is turned which is fixed with the clutch outer as one unit.
   c. On the rotor is fixed on the crankshaft by a key of 4 mm. rotation of the clutch outer is transmitted on the crankshaft.
   d. The starting clutch roller spring is useful for smooth running of roller without any irregular meshing.
   Furthermore a spring cap is used to make smooth motions of the starting clutch roller spring and the roller.
2. When the engine starts running
   a. Rotational spped of the crankshaft becomes faster than that of the sprocket.
   b. Transmission from the starting motor is cut, due to centrifugal force on the roller which presses the spring and moves to the wider space of the clutch outer-

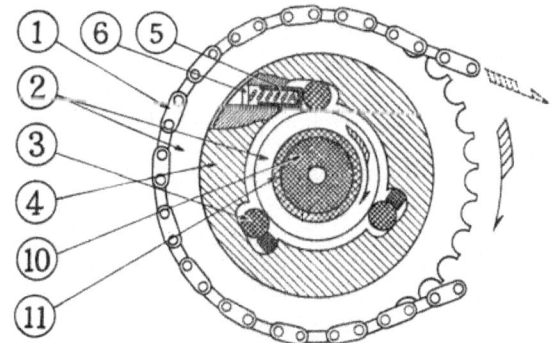

Fig. 11-42. Picture showing principle of function of the overrunning clutch (A)

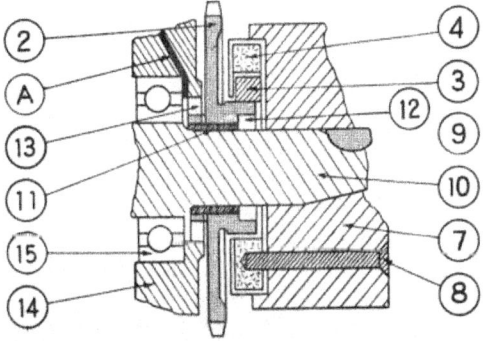

Fig. 11-43. Picture showing principle of function of the overrunning clutch (B)

3. Lubrication

   Lubrications for the over running clutch is done by oil dropped through the hole (A) in the Figure which passes through the groove at three parts (B) and stays inside of the inner oil seal 2035 of 20 mm bush and the lock oil seal 326575 to prevent burning.

   Therefore after diassembly it is necessary to clean oil holes (A) and (B) by compressed air.

4. Precuation about Maintenance

   As Life of the over running clutch depends on the function of roller, special attention is needed for its handling.

   a) grease put on the roller should be used designated one. (Part No. 719111. silicon grease)

   This designated grease have several features, ie, high resistant to cold and hot (−40°C∼200°C), least variation for frictions coefficients due to temperature and other variation.

   Before putting this grease on, cleanse each part by gasoline, and after drying up, paint grease thinly all over the surface of the roller.

   b. Be careful about magnetic force.

   Not only roller or roller spring, but also parts around the clutch should be avoided from magnetizing. Any tiny resistance will unfavorably affect smooth running of roller.

No.	Part name	Quantity	No.	Part name	Quantity
1	Starting chain	1	8	Cross hole screw	3
2	Starting sprocket	1	9	Half mooh key (large)	1
3	Roller	3	10	R-crank shaft	1
4	Clutch outer	1	11	Bush	1
5	Starting clutch roller spring cup	3	12	20305 oil seal	1
			13	326275 lock oil seal	1
6	Starting clutch roller spring	3	14	R crank bearing housing	1
7	AC dynamo rotor	1	15	Z bearing	1

F. Starter magnetic switch

Current to rotate the starting motor will reach about 100 A. To reduce resistance big wire is needed, and also the switch to make on or off should be larger size at the contacting part. Accordingly it will be difficult to find such place as easy to operate switch feeding current directly on the starting motor.

In such cases, switch utilizing magneto can be equipped at the most convenient place between the battery and the starting motor and put the switch to operate this magneto separately to make possible remote control with least current.

1. **Principle of function**

    a) If current flows on the primary side, an electromagnet actuates to attract iron core resisting spring force.

    b) The contact point at the end of the iron core connects the secondary circuit. (Fig. 11-46).

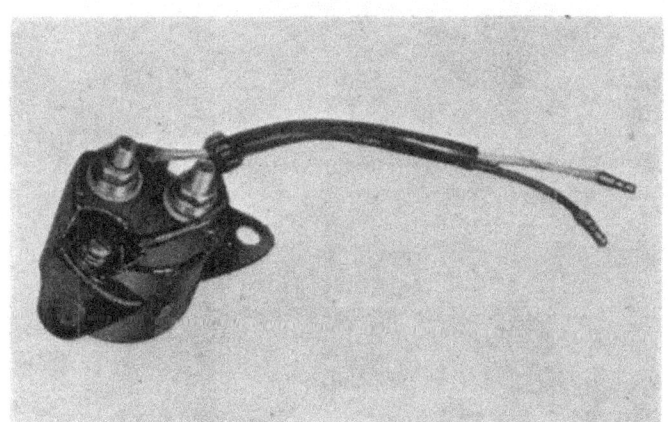

Fig. 11-45. Starter magnetic switch

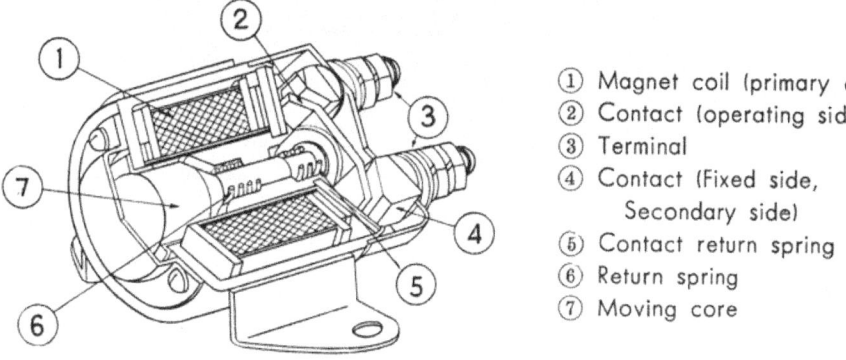

① Magnet coil (primary coil)
② Contact (operating side)
③ Terminal
④ Contact (Fixed side, Secondary side)
⑤ Contact return spring
⑥ Return spring
⑦ Moving core

Fig. 11-46. Construction of starter magnetic switch

2. **Precaution**

    a) When put voltage of 12 V between both terminal of the primary circuit, if heard clicking sound, the contact point of the primary circuit is connected.

b) If used for a long time, contact point gets wear and damage to increase resistance, and sometimes no current flows. (even if sound of clicking is heard, sometimes the cell motor forced to stop). In such cases, disassemble it and polish the contact point with a file or a sand paper. To disassemble take this switch from the body.

c. Operational current on the primary side less than 12 V, 3.5 A. (Fig. 11–47, 11–48)

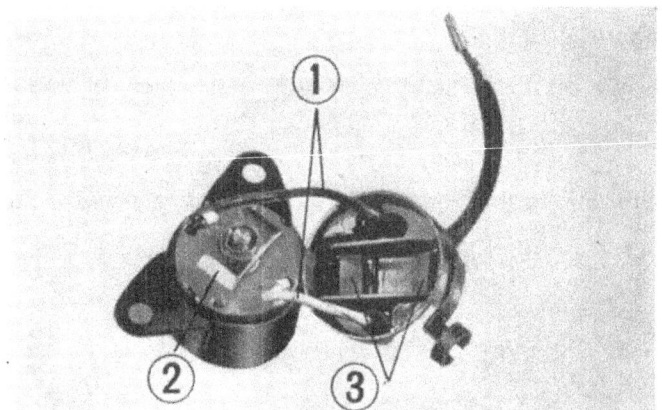

Fig. 11–47. Disassembly of magnetic switch (cap is opened)

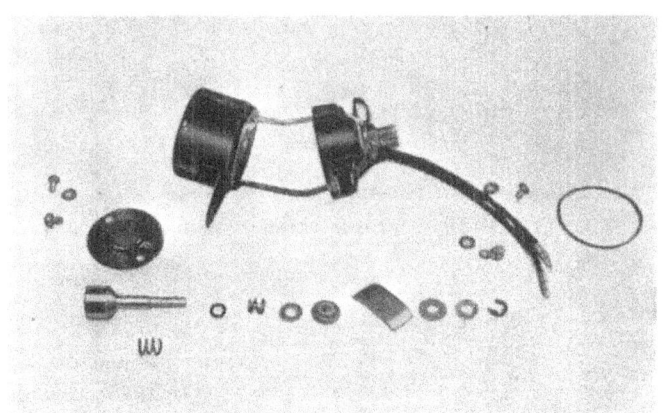

Fig. 11–48. Disassembly of magnetic switch (assemble part)

3. PARTS FOR USE OF SAFE GUARD

Speedmeter, Tachometer

For Model C 72, 77 is equipped only a speedmeter but not a tachometer.

The speedmeter is generally magnetic type, and rotation proportional to that of the wheel is transmitted to the speedmeter by means of a flexible cable.

For the tachometer, magnetic tachometer is used alike the speedmeter and rotation proportional to that of the camshaft in the cylinder head is transmitted to the tachometer. (Fig. 11-49).

Fig. 11-49. Speedo-tachometer

Fig. 11-50. Dial of Speedo-tachometer

The speedmeter is consisted of speed indicator and distance meter, and speed is expressed by km/h, and running distance is integrated up to 99.999 km by the distance meter.

The tachometer shows revolution number per minute by indicator (r.p.m). Constructionally it is same type with speedmeter and stored in the same case of the speedmeter.

Only different points are that no integration mechanism and different sign and measures on the dial plate.

Construction of the speedmeter and tachometer is shown in the figure.

The magnets rotates with same rotational speed with that of the flexible cable and the induction disk (of aluminum or Copper made) moves with indicator as one unit.

The magnet shelter disk furnishes magnetic field to generate eddy current on the disk by the rotating magnet.

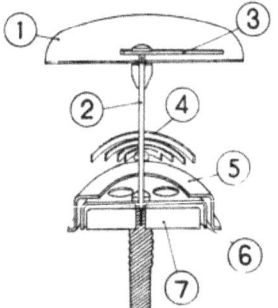

① Dial
② Induction dish axis
③ Indicator
④ Hair spring
⑤ Magnet shelter disk (charcoal disk)
⑥ Induction disk
⑦ Magneto

Fig. 11-51. Principle of speedmeter

Fig. 11-52. Parts of Speedometer

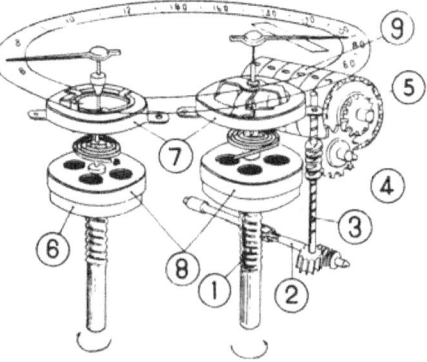

① No. 1 shaft
② No. 2 shaft
③ No. 3 shaft
④ No. 4 shaft
⑤ No. 5 shaft
⑥ Magneto
⑦ Magneto shelter disk
⑧ Indication disk
⑨ Total

Fig. 11-53. Construction of total distance meter

By means of this eddy current the magnet shelter disk is moved by proportional revolving force to the magnet and indicator shows on the dial balancing with reaction of the correctly adjusted hair spring.

When the can is stopped, (on the tachometer, engine is stopped) the indicator and the induction disk come back to the zero by restoring force of the hair spring.

For the speedmeter revolution of the front wheel is reduced in the gear box, and the cable turns 1400 revolutions per 1 km running, on the other hand for the tachometer, revolution of the cam shaft is reduced further.

Reduction ratio of the tachometer axis to the crank shaft is 3:20. (Fig. 11-52).

<u>Total distance meter</u>
reduction

JIS Regulation

Type	Flexible Shaft	reduction ratio	Speed meter indication
two or tri wheel car	1 400	1/1 400	60 km/h
4-wheel car	637	1/637	60 km/h

The distance meter is shown constructionally on Fig. 11-53, the magnet shaft cutted worm on it transmit its rotation as No. 2→shaft No. 3→shaft No. 4→wheel No. 5 wheel reducing each speed.

On the dial of the total distance meter figures as 0, 1, 2 . . . 9 are marked, and teeth are cut so as to rotate each wheel for one turn, the succeeding wheel rotates $1/10$ revolution. (Fig. 11-53).

MEMO

TROUBLE SHOOTING

TROUBLE SHOOTING

Procedures of diagnosis for finding out causes of trouble and their probable causes are discribed as follows:

1. **Engine does not start or hard to start**

    (1) Remove the carburetter float chamber and check for fuel flow, if fuel is not supplied enough;

    1-1. Clogged fuel line
    1-2. Clogged fuel tank cap vent hole
    1-3. Clogged fuel cock
    1-4. Clogged carburetter line or stuck needle valve

    (2) Remove the spark plugs, attach them to the spark plug caps, turn in the ignition switch and rotate the crank shaft with starter motor while the (−) electrods are grounded. If the spark plugs do not spark well or nil;

    2-1. Faulty spark plug, (to make sure, check the spark plug with spark plug tester.)
    2-2. Sooty or wet spark plug
    2-3. Contact breaker point
    2-4. Faulty condenser
    2-5 Incorrect adjustment of contact breaker point
    2-6. Short circuit or breakage in ignition coil or wiring
    2-7. Damaged combination switch

    (3) Check compression pressure at the cylinder with a compression gauge and if lack or nil of compression is indicated in either cylinder;

    3-1. Incorrect tappet clearance
    3-2. Incorrect seating of valves in valve seats
    3-3. Excessive wear in valve
    3-4. Excessive wear in piston ring, piston cylinder
    3-5. Blown out cylinder head gasket
    3-6. Seized valve in valve guide
    3-7. Faulty valve timing

    (4) Start engine following the procedure of starting but engine seems to start but won't continue running;

    4-1. Too wide opened choke shutter in cold weather
    4-2. Wide opened air screw of carburetter adjusting air-screw
    4-3. Damaged carburetter insulator or gasket

2. **Engine does not develope full power**

   (1) Stand the vehicle on the main stand and rotate the rear wheel by hand when the gear is set in neutral, if wheel does not turn easily;

       1-1. Dragging rear brake-incorrect adjustment

       1-2. Damaged wheel bearing

       1-3. Too tight drive chain tension, in correct adjustment

   (2) Check the tyre air pressure and inflate to the specific amount.

   (3) Check the clutch for slip and if it is found slipping;

       3-1. Improper adjustment of clutch

       3-2. Worn clutch facing

       3-3. Weakened clutch springs

   (4) Measure the highest revolutions of crankshaft with a revolution counter and if the engine does not develope full revolution;

       4-1. Choked carburetter at somewhere

       4-2. Clogged air cleaner

       4-3. Insufficient supply of fuel to the intake

       4-4. Clogged muffler

       4-5. Faulty ignition coil or contact breaker points

       4-6. Faulty seating of valve

       4-7. Incorrect ignition timing

       4-8. Excess weak valve springs

       4-9. Faulty spark plug; test the spark plug with spark plug tester

   (5) Check oil level in the crankcase and adjust the level to the specification, or excess amount of oil result in the trouble.

   (6) Inspect for excess heating of engine and if found it same;

       6-1. Excess carbon deposit in combustion chamber

       6-2. Inferior grade of fuel is used

       6-3. Slippery clutch

       6-4. Lean air-fuel mixture; improper size of main jet in carburetter

       6-5. Dirty cylinder and cylinder head

   (7) Check for the engine developing or knocking when it submit to quick acceleration or successive running at high speed and if it is so; The probable causes are same as No. (6).

3. **Engine runs erratic and/or with miss firing**
    (1) Adjust air screw of carburetter properly and still runs under same circumstances.
        1-1. Faulty ignition timing
        1-2. Damaged carburetter insulator or packing
        1-3. Faulty spark plug
        1-4. Faulty condenser
        1-5. Faulty ignition coil
        1-6. Faulty contact breaker point
        1-7. Incorrect tappet clearance
    (2) Check for missing at high speed and if the engine is still under the same.
        2-1. Insufficient supply of fuel
        2-2. Incorrect valve timing
        2-3. Damaged or weak valve springs
        2-4. Other causes mentioned in No. (1)

4. **Excessive oil consumption or exhaust blue or black smoke**
    (1) If the engine exhausts smoke while continuous running at high or low RPM.
        1-1. Worn cylinder or piston rings
        1-2. Reversely assembled rings in piston
        1-3. Excess clearance between exhaust valve and guide
    (2) If the engine exhausts smoke just after when closing throttle valve suddenly from certain opening ;
        2-1. Excess clearance between inlet valve and guide
        2-2. Clogged air vent hole or plastic tube

5. **Clutch jerks or engages unsmoothly**
    (1) If the machine moves off with jerking or the engine stops at the moment when the clutch engaged.
        1-1. Uneven tensions of clutch springs
        1-2. Distorted clutch plates or facings
        1-3. Sticky movement of clutch plate in the clutch outer

6. **Gear shifting does not operate correctly**
    (1) When the changing gear does not engage.
        1-1. Worn notch on the shift drum
        1-2. Stuck shift fork to the shift drum
        1-3. Worn shift fork

(2) If the gear jumps out while running;
    2-1. Worn dogs on the gear shifter
    2-2. Worn or distorted shift fork
    2-3. Weakened shift drum stopper spring

7. **Engine runs with unusual noise when the tappet clearances assumed correctly:**

  (1) If knocking noise is heard from cylinder when accelerating engine.
      1-1. Excess clearance between cylinder and piston

  (2) If chattering noise is heard even if the cam chain has been adjusted;
      2-1. Excess worn cam chain
      2-2. Excess worn cam chain tensioner spring or roller

  (3) When knocking noise is heard from crank case.
      3-1. Worn crank shaft big end
      3-2. Worn crank shaft bearing

  (4) If the clutch incures noise when operating clutch lever.
      4-1. Excess clearance between the clutch plate and clutch outer
      4-2. Excess clearance between the clutch center and clutch plate

8. **Troubles in steering**

  (1) If it is felt that the steering is hard at turning;
      1-1. Over-tight steering ball races
      1-2. Damaged steering
      1-3. Bent steering stem

  (2) Steering wanders or pull to one side while running.
      2-1. Worn front and/or rear wheel bearing
      2-2. Distorted front and/or rear wheel rim
      2-3. Loose spokes
      2-4. Worn rear fork pivot bushing or front arm pivot bushing
      2-5. Bent front fork or frame or rear fork
      2-6. Incorrect rear wheel alignment
      3-7. Uneven strength of cushion springs on both side

9. **Troubles of brakes**

  (1) The brake does not actuate properly even after the free play is adjusted correctly.
      1-1. Worn brake shoes

1-2. Worn brake cam

1-3. Worn brake pedal shaft

1-4 Brake shoe contaminated with oil or water

1-5. Stuck brake cable or rear brake link

1-6. Lack of grease in brake cam

(2) Brake squeaks when applied.

2-1. Excess worn brake shoe

2-2. Contaminated surface of brake shoe

2-3. Warped or pitted wall of brake drum

2-4. Excess wear of brake panel spacer

MEMO

OTHER CLASSIC MOTORCYCLE MANUALS CURRENTLY AVAILABLE IN THIS SERIES:

TRIUMPH 1935-1939 MAINTENANCE & REPAIR MANUAL

All Pre-War single & twin cylinder models: L2/1, 2/1, 2/5, 3/1, 3/2, 3/5, 5/1, 5/2, 5/3, 5/4, 5/5, 5/10, 6/1, Tiger 70, Tiger 80, Tiger 90, 2H, Tiger 70C, 3S, 3H, Tiger 80C, 5H, Tiger 90C, 6S, 2HC, 3SC, 5T Speed Twin, 5S and T100 Tiger 100.

Much of the data is applicable to earlier models that utilize the following engines: *Single Cylinder:* 250cc OHV, 350cc SV, 350cc OHV, 500cc SV, 500cc OHV, 550cc SV and 600cc SV. *Twin Cylinder:* 500cc OHV and 650cc OHV.

TRIUMPH 1937-1951 WORKSHOP MANUAL (A. St. J. Masters)

The most comprehensive Workshop Manual available for pre swing-arm Triumph motorcycles. Covers rigid frame and sprung hub single cylinder SV & OHV and twin cylinder OHV pre-war, military, and post-war models: 2H, Tiger 70, Tiger 70C, 3S, 3H, Tiger 80, Tiger 80C, 5H, Tiger 90, Tiger 90C, 6S, 2HC, 3SC, 5T Speed Twin, 5S, T100 Tiger 100, 3HW, 3SW, 5SW, 3T, Grand Prix, TR5 Trophy and 6T Thunderbird.

Much of the data is applicable to earlier models that utilize the following engines: *Single Cylinder:* 250cc OHV, 350cc SV, 350cc OHV, 500cc SV, 500cc OHV and 600cc SV. *Twin Cylinder:* 350cc OHV, 500cc OHV and 650cc OHV.

TRIUMPH 1945-1955 FACTORY WORKSHOP MANUAL NO.11

The most comprehensive Workshop Manual available for pre-unit, twin-cylinder Triumph motorcycles. Covers the full line of rigid frame, sprung hub, swing-arm and 350cc models: 5T Speed Twin, T100 Tiger 100, TR5 Trophy, 6T Thunderbird, T110 Tiger 110 and 3T De-Luxe.

Much of the data is applicable to later models that utilize the following engines: Twin Cylinder 350cc OHV, 500cc OHV and 650cc OHV.

BMW FACTORY WORKSHOP MANUAL R50, R50S, R60, R69S

A reproduction of the factory workshop manual for the R50, R50S, R60, R69S twin cylinder series of BMW's. Also included is a supplement for the USA models: R50US, R60US, R69US.

The text and illustration captions are printed in English, German, French and Spanish and while the translations may at times be a little quirky, the data is comprehensive and invaluable to the BMW enthusiast.

BMW FACTORY WORKSHOP MANUAL R27, R28

A reproduction of the factory workshop manual for the R27 and R28 single cylinder series of BMW's, while quite scarce in the USA these were very popular models in Europe.

The text and illustration captions are printed in English, German, French and Spanish and while the translations may at times be a little quirky, the data is comprehensive and invaluable to the BMW enthusiast.

NORTON FACTORY TWIN CYLINDER WORKSHOP MANUAL 1957-1970

A reproduction of the factory workshop manual for both the *Lightweight Twins:* 250cc Jubilee, 350cc Navigator and 400cc Electra and the *Heavyweight Twins:* Model 77, 88, 88SS, 99, 99SS, Sports Special, Manxman, Mercury, Atlas, G15, P11, N15, Ranger (P11A) which makes this manual appropriate for all Norton models that utilized this series of 500, 600, 650 and 750cc engines through the 1970 model year.

NORTON MAINTENANCE & REPAIR MANUAL 1932-1939

All Pre-War SV, OHV and OHC models: 16H, 16I, 18, 19, 20, 50, 55, ES2, CJ, CSI, International 30 & 40

VINCENT WORKSHOP MANUAL 1935-1955

All Series A, B & C Models

ARIEL WORKSHOP MANUAL 1933-1951
All Single, Twin & 4 cylinder models

HONDA FACTORY WORKSHOP MANUAL
250 & 305cc C.72 C.77 CS.72, CS.77, CB.72, CB.77 [HAWK]

OTHER CLASSIC MOTORCYCLE MANUALS COMING SOON IN THIS SAME SERIES:

ARIEL MAINTENANCE & REPAIR MANUAL 1932-1939
LF3, LF4, LG, NF3, NF4, NG, OG, VA, VA3, VA4, VB, VF3, VF4, VG,
Red Hunter LH, NH, OH, VH & Square Four 4F, 4G, 4H

BRIDGESTONE FACTORY WORKSHOP MANUAL
50 Sport, 60 Sport, 90 De Luxe, 90 Trail, 90 Mountain, 90 Sport,
175 Dual Twin & Hurricane

DUCATI OHC FACTORY WORKSHOP MANUAL
160 Junior Monza, 250 Monza, 250 GT, 250 Mark 3,
250 Mach 1, 250 SCR & 350 Sebring

HONDA FACTORY WORKSHOP MANUAL
125 & 150cc C.92, CS.92, CB.92, C.95 & CA.95

HONDA FACTORY WORKSHOP MANUAL
50cc ~ 100, 110, C.100 & C.110

HONDA MAINTENANCE & REPAIR MANUAL 1960-1964
50cc ~ C.100, C.102, C.110 & C.114
125cc C.92 & CB.92 – 250cc C.72 & CB.72

SUZUKI FACTORY WORKSHOP MANUAL 250/200cc
T10, T20 [X-6 Hustler] T200 [X-5 Invader & Sting Ray]

VESPA MAINTENANCE & REPAIR MANUAL 1946-1959
All 125cc & 150cc models including 42/L2 & Gran Sport

VILLIERS ENGINE WORKSHOP MANUAL
All Villiers engines and ancillaries through 1947

BRITISH MILITARY MAINTENANCE & REPAIR MANUAL
Service & Repair data for all British WD motorcycles

BRITISH MOTORCYCLE ENGINES
AJS, Ariel, BSA, Excelsior, JAP, Norton, Royal Enfield, Rudge, Scott, Sunbeam, Triumph, Velocette,
Villiers & Vincent ~ a compilation of 1950's articles from
The Motor Cycle dealing with engine design.

PLEASE CHECK OUR WEBSITE OR CONTACT YOUR DEALER FOR AVAILABILITY
~ WWW.VELOCEPRESS.COM ~

www.ingramcontent.com/pod-product-compliance
Lightning Source LLC
Chambersburg PA
CBHW060252240426
43673CB00047B/1912